THE
Black Father
PERSPECTIVE

What We
Want America
to Know

COMPILED BY
KIMMOLY K. LABOO

ISBN-13: 978-1-7351126-2-6
Library of Congress Control Number: 2020909872

For information regarding special discounts for bulk purchases, please contact the publisher: LaBoo Publishing Enterprise, LLC
staff@laboopublishing.com
www.laboopublishing.com

Table of Contents

THE BLACK FATHER PERSPECTIVE
WHAT WE WANT AMERICA TO KNOW

Introduction

I wanted to know what black men thought and felt, so I decided to ask them. As the visionary for this work it was important for me to share my vision with these men then step back and let them be, which is often hard for a black woman to do. This was a humbling experience, trying to find the balance between being structured and supportive, yet not nagging. It was quite the challenge. However, it was worth it. The skewed narrative in America would have us believe that black fathers aren't present. I know for a fact that's not entirely true. There are plenty of black men who love, care for and provide for their children and I wanted to provide a platform for them to share their perspective.

As a wounded black woman, throughout my life, I often attracted wounded black men. In reality, I was a wounded girl trying to fix the broken men I encountered. I realize now the impact of not having my father in my life and how it played a part in the men I subconsciously sought out. My definition of love was tainted by the love I didn't receive from my father as a child. Because I was left unprotected and fatherless as a young girl, I was always attracted to men who were large in stature because I was looking for a protector. While I accomplished that and they were able to protect me physically, they were not able to care for me emotionally, nor should they have been expected to. For as broken as my relationships have been with black men, I always saw the good in them. I saw their desire to love, protect, and provide the best way they knew how.

For more than 30 years of my life I longed for my father. It was my writing that brought us together in my adult years. I had approximately three good years with him before he took his last breath. Those three years changed my life forever. The impact of a father in the life of his child is immeasurable; you will see that magnified throughout the pages of this book.

The accounts of love, strength, honor and legacy that are shared will give a glimpse of what fatherhood looks like from the black male perspective. I am honored to present such heartfelt testimonies of what it looks like to be a black father in America.

"Father' is the noblest title
a man can be given.
It is more than a biological
role. It signifies a patriarch,
a leader, an exemplar,
a confidant, a teacher,
a hero, a friend."

Robert L. Backman

Mr. Jason A. Woodford Sr., a husband, father of 5, US. Army Veteran, musician, and minister, he is also a School-based and Community Mental Health Therapist through C&C Advocacy, Inc. and Building Blocks HealthCare Network at Belmont Elementary. Part-time, he is a Direct Care Worker at Positive Steps, LLC, Psychiatric Rehabilitation Program. Jason also worked at the Maryland Board of Social Work Examiners for four years in the Compliance Unit. He obtained a Bachelor's in theology from Amora Theological Institute (2015). He received his Bachelor's in social work from Coppin State University (2016). During his tenure at Coppin, Jason served as the Vice President of Theta Rho (2016-17), as well as inducted into Social Work, Psychology and Social Science Honors Society, and was an inaugural intern of the Dorothy Height Center for Social Justice, functioning as the Faith and Communities Coordinator. Mr. Woodford obtained his Advanced Standing master's in social work from University of Maryland, Baltimore (2017). Mr. Woodford is also an alumnus of the esteemed 2016-2017 Council on Social Work Education Minority Fellowship cohort, Licensed Mental Health Therapist, and a Certified Mental Health First Aid Provider.

Mr. Woodford has over 20 years of experience serving urban youth and families within faith communities and is now dedicated to providing clinical services to underserved populations to decrease the stigma of mental health. To that end, he dreams of opening his own PRP, Substance Use outpatient program, and Outpatient Mental Health Clinic called, 90 Degree, LLC. in the fall of 2020.

DADDY MADE THE DIFFERENCE

JASON A. WOODFORD

• • • • • • • • • • • • •

Introduction

I finally had my day to enjoy a respite from the usual demands that come from being a husband, father, minister, friend, and therapist. It came after many days of silently requesting time off from the always-demanding taskmaster called Life, only to be reminded of the reality that it's never really granted, because you must be prepared to show up any time Life calls. I'm aware that these demands are not exclusive to us men, as I have seen many women, whether by choice or circumstances beyond their control, answer when Life called. Hmm, that's interesting— both men and women get the call, so what makes the male experience or perspective so different? Could it be how we were taught to pick up the phone? When the phone rang, some of us answered, "Who dis, who you lookin' for?" while others answered, "Hello, how can I help you?" For most of us it was likely somewhere in between, but my premise is that how we respond to the calls and experiences that life brings may have someone else's thumbprint attached to it, like an iPhone. So the question is who is answering our calls? Whether it's Sunday brunch mimosas with the girls, all-night prayer meeting at church, twerking something in the club, or on the prowl like hyenas in the African Serengeti looking for fresh prey, the sobering reality is that how we "answer" is tied to a place, a person, or often a problem.

As I consider fatherhood, from the perspective of a Black man in America, there's almost a sense of resistance from within. As a therapist, I wonder if this is the same feeling that a client would feel in their initial session? Like Tom Cruise's character Ethan Hunt in the blockbuster movie series *Mission Impossible*, there's a new mission in front of me, but in order to accomplish it, it begs the question, "Can I be me, or will I have to wear a disguise?"

Lying on the couch, in mismatched socks and a wrinkled shirt, with a remote in my hand, I experience a sense of solace in the productivity of an empty "baby-can you, Daddy-can you, Jason-can you" list. As I passively watch television my mind has the chance to defragment like an old computer, putting memories and files in their respective places for faster retrieval. I chuckle internally, as memories of my father peek their heads like a turtle just above the surface of my mind and quickly tuck away, just to let me know that they are there. As I pet my own turtles, Yoshi and Shishi, I come closer to those memories and engage in the invitation to explore and share with you what they want me to see.

The Moment

On the stage of life, the house curtains of self-awareness open at the age of five. There's laughing, playing, and a symphony of aromas that say, "I am glad you are here." It was a familiar feeling; as if by design, my default setting was love. I didn't have to learn it or be taught it; I was trusting, accepting and free. It was my birthday! Clowns, balloons, friends, Mom, Dad, brothers, and sisters—this was family; this was safety; this was love. Then, I didn't know to call it love. I only knew the feeling I had at the moment was congruent with the feelings I had for those around me. This should be our desire, that we paint on the canvas of children's hearts the signature message to them, "I am glad you are here" before we correct them or chastise them. When they look at us, can they see in our eyes that we are glad they are here? Even in the absence of the trinkets of materialism that we sometimes use as surrogates for, rather than extensions of our affection, can they feel that we are glad that they are here?

In common with most individuals, my childhood experiences were not linear or static, but very dynamic, often dramatic, and in some cases traumatic. "Happy birthday, dear Jason! Happy birthday to yooou!" (singing). This was a pivotal moment of validation and belonging. Take note that the power of the party is in the people who attend. That's why invitations are so important, because they indicate your presence alone would enhance the experience of the one being celebrated. The invitation substantiates the principle of relationship and community, that the completeness of our human experience is tied to our connection to one another. This moment agreed with my default setting. I was aware that everyone was together, and everyone was happy. In my young mind, a belief system was being established in a very conscious way that said this is how it was supposed to be.

Almost equally as important as the feeling of being celebrated was how you felt when the party was over. The clown did his last trick, one by one my friends were picked up by their parents, and my mother and other family members wrapped up leftover cake and food. I was ecstatic, as if I'd just watched the finale of the Fourth of July fireworks, rehearsing the memories that were made that day with family and friends. But then something happened. The toys were put away, the gifts were organized, and my father hugged and kissed me and said that he was about to go home. For some reason, the joy of that day began to fade. I felt a knot in my throat as I hugged him back and said "okay," but deep down I wanted to go with him, deep down I wanted him to stay. It was in that *moment* things began to change. Something in me wanted to be with my father, but I didn't know why… Time would tell…

1. What were your happiest times in childhood?
2. What were your saddest times?
3. Have you identified when your "moment" happened?
4. Have you identified when your child/children's "moment" happened?
5. Mom or Dad, how has the "moment" impacted your relationship with your child/children?
6. Whose voice do you hear when you answer the calls of Life?
7. Do you trust that voice?

The Model

It's 1979, a man buries his wife of 30 years due to illness. Six children—two boys and four girls—mourn the loss of their mother, along with three grandchildren. The minister gives the last rites and commits this wife, mother, daughter, sister, grandmother back to the earth, prays a blessing of comfort for the family and sends them home to continue the grieving process with other grieving family and friends.

Remember I asked you, "Who answers when life calls?" Well, a story was shared with me about a young 27-year-old woman walking with her cousin one day when a car pulled up, and a man with salt and pepper hair, smelling like goodness and mercy, got out of the car and approached her. As a man myself, I can understand him seeing such beauty that he just had to approach to acknowledge it. If you ask me, I will tell you the woman, especially the **black** woman, is the most beautiful creature on this planet. Her hair, her skin, her femininity—King Solomon took it further and said, "Your lips drip nectar; honey and milk are under your tongue." Lord have mercy! I love it—so much so that I married one. We'll get to that later; I digress. As I mentioned, I can understand the man approaching this red-haired, dimpled-cheek black woman, but "Sir, didn't you just bury your wife?"

I wasn't there to hear the conversation that was shared on that day, but nine months later, in June 1980, that conversation led to a son named Jason. I will certainly not attempt to psychoanalyze my father, or judge/condemn how I got here, one reason being I never lost a spouse, and also, I've experienced and have seen the arrogance of youth as they judge the elders for what's lingering in them as well. Do you know what's in your model?

In hindsight my father having me when he was 51 years old gave me some advantages, in that he had 28 or so years of experience raising children before I got here. He was beyond the trial-and-error stage of parenting. I already had two adult brothers in the military and four sisters who were already married with children and in established careers. I was truly the baby; I was their baby. To this very day, they still love me like I'm little baby brother Jason.

My father had life experience; at 51 years old he had established himself as a voice for labor workers with the Teamsters Club, Local 557, here in Baltimore. He was a man's man. He believed in looking sharp all the time. He was the guy who shaved and showered just to go to the supermarket. One day I asked him why he had to do all of that. He looked at me, grinned and replied, "You never know who you may meet." His favorite cologne was JOVAN-Sex Appeal. They should have called it "nine months later;" it was some good-smelling stuff.

My father didn't have to administer corporal punishment, in our vernacular "whip your behind." My father told me, "Why should I have to beat you when I have the power? If you don't listen to what I say, I'll just cut off your privileges because you will need me to do something." Fathers should teach their sons how to use their power appropriately. All along he was teaching me the power of appearance, the power of scent and the power of money. In my father's house, it was clear who was in charge, who had the last say, not from a dictatorial stance of fear and anxiety but one of respect and responsibility. It's easy to submit to a benevolent king. This is true for women as well, not only children.

I'll never forget, I was acting out in class and it had been going on for some time. My father, not prescribing to the route of corporal punishment, took a more cerebral approach. He picked me up after school; at this point I was in the fourth grade. Instead of going the usual route home, he drove to a part of the city that I had never been in or seen before. He pulled over as if he were about to make a kingpin drug drop and cut the car off. He didn't say anything for a minute. It seemed like the silence in the car had sound, and in my periphery, I saw him observing the individuals who were on the corner selling drugs, leaning in the gutter, totally oblivious to our presence, and with his deep Lion-King Mufasa voice, he broke the silence and said, "Do you see them over there?"

I said, "Yes."

He continued, "The way the world works is people who live that kind of lifestyle will one day die, but somebody has to take their place to keep it going. Will it be you?"

At that moment I knew that I didn't want to be on the street, and I knew that selling drugs was bad in my nine-year-old world. But my father was making a connection between my behavior, education and those individuals who were strung out and selling drugs. In a greater message, looking back, my father was not just trying to get me to be good in school, but he was planting a seed in my mind to look at the greater context as a black male who, even in the fourth grade, could be inadvertently preparing himself to replace the man or woman who is trying to numb the pain of past failures and traumas with a needle in the arm. Fathers should expose their children to reality, even if it means exposing their own, while protecting the possibility of their child's success. Every good father wants to see his child experience a life he may have only dreamed of.

However, that was not the case in my earlier years with my mother. When I was born my mother only had nine years of experience parenting with my older brother from another relationship and, unbeknownst to me, years of unresolved childhood trauma and relational abuse.

As I describe my experience as a young boy, I want to preface my words by saying that regardless of what I share relating to my childhood experience with my mother, I will never dishonor her or diminish her dignity as my mother. She gave me life, and I love her and have always honored her. Love you, Ma!

Now, growing up on the corner of Bonner and Wolcott could be a Lifetime Biopic all by itself. It was a dramatic and traumatic place. It was there that I had my "moment" at the age of five, after my birthday: Something inside me knew I should be with my father. It wasn't too long after that birthday party that the message of "I'm glad you are here" began to change to "Why are you here?" This little mind and body could only take so many verbal and physical blows. This resulted in bed-wetting that triggered more beatings and ridicule, causing little innocent Jason to start covering up his "wrongdoing" (bed-wetting), hiding urine-stained sheets and underwear because telling the truth meant pain. No one took into consideration that bed-wetting is a trauma response.

Mothers and fathers, when we fail to examine the *why*, we run the risk of incorrectly dealing with the *what*. Looking back, my mother connected my bed-wetting to me, in essence, turning me into the problem, and in order to get rid of the problem she had to get rid of me. Or was my bed-wetting the issue at all? As with my father, I will not psychoanalyze my mother or condemn her either, but it begs the question for parents who read this, how often do our children suffer as a result of our unresolved pain, because we won't answer the *whys* of our own lives?

As I grew older, the abuse continued and escalated for me and my older brother, but I won't tell his story. My mother began to chip away at the core of who I was, and the only thing that I knew for sure was I was supposed to be with my daddy. She would say things, like, "Your father doesn't want you; the only reason you're here is because he's retired and wants to go on cruises and enjoy his life." However, every time I called him, with open arms he let me stay with him for a few days at a time, throughout the week, and all I experienced was "I am glad you're here." Brothers and sisters, that knowing and feeling of belonging transcends any toy, video, or material possession. One thing you cannot do is lie to a child about how you feel about them. It's biological, it's essence, it's spirit. They know before you give them the gift. The greatest gift is you first.

At the age of nine I got a respite from the trauma of living in my mother's house. For one whole year I was where I belonged, just me and my daddy. At that time, I was spending time with my sisters Sheila, Shenetta, Yvette, and Yvonne and brothers Boo-Boo and Ronald. I had a whole family, I had my father, and a couple of my sisters were around the same age as my mother, so that was covered.

Then one day my father picked me up from school; the summer was ahead of me and I was looking forward to spending time with my grandmother, swimming, going to church, and reading the book of Proverbs with her, when he told me my mother wanted me to move to Georgia with her and my little brothers on her side, Brandon, Aaron and Ryan. My father asked me how I felt about it, and he could tell that I wasn't happy. I could tell that he wasn't happy either, because he hugged me and said, "I'll come down there and visit, and you'll come up here for the summer." Fathers, fight for your children.

From ages 10 to 16, the trauma resurfaced, because you can move to another state, country, or world for that matter, but if the same you shows up… you can finish that thought. I must be honest: It wasn't all bad; however, the bad was enough to do significant damage to my emotional and psychological wellbeing. I was no longer afraid of the beatings. Years of verbal and physical abuse had hardened little Jason, whose memory of that fifth birthday party seemed to fade into oblivion.

Mothers, in situations where your child lives with you, you have the awesome responsibility and opportunity to shape the narrative of the father to that child. Either you can birth a determination in that child to be greater than the failures of his/her father, or you can plant a seed of hate for the other half of who they are. Remember, if a child hates his mother or father, they will hate a part of themselves.

At age sixteen, I came back home to my mother's house after being gone for two weeks at a church friend's house. I had no fear of consequences. My mother attempted to secure her weapon of choice for discipline, the brown leather belt. She commenced to hitting me and I looked her directly in her eye without a tear or emotion. The look she gave me, I suspect, was an indication that the Jason she knew had left the building, and at that moment she said, "You have to go with your father."

Mothers and fathers across America and around the world, I understand how difficult it may be, if possible at all in some instances, to produce a positive relationship with your child's father or mother; however, if the opportunity for that child to connect to that parent is open, it may be difficult in the beginning when you call on the help of the one you've trained your child to hate.

The Man

It was the summer of '96. I was back home with my father. Through those six years he did come to Georgia to visit me, but he left me. I did come to Baltimore to visit for the summer, but I had to go back, carrying the toxic narrative of a hurting mother who still hadn't engaged her *why*, thus all her *whats* were misaligned. Social relationships began to wane, giving way to conflict with old comrades and failed relationships. At least I was with my father, but every year I came to visit, I was coming back with another layer of hardened skin that could not get the moisturizing nourishment of love that softens the soul. Conversations with my father were general and superficial. I could tell that he was glad I was home, but that didn't penetrate the parts of me that were hardened. I left the house to spend time with old neighborhood friends until the evening and came in to have dinner and go to my room to watch television. That was pretty much the whole summer, until school started.

Until one day I came home from school, Forest Park High School, home of the Foresters, with no expectation of anything special. I came in the house, checked the fridge, dropped my book bag, and then went upstairs—my normal routine. As I was making my way up the steps to my room, I saw my father on the bed in my peripheral vision, so I spoke. "Hey Ar," which was what I called him, the first two letters of his name. My brothers and sisters called him Arthur, but for some reason it just didn't feel right calling my father by his first name, so I made an abbreviated version, and he accepted it.

He called me to his room, and he had a laminated sheet of paper in his hand, I was familiar with his handwriting so I could see it was some kind of letter. He pulled me close to him and with tears in his eyes, he looked at me and said, "Do you know how much I love you?" Shocked by the moment and the expression of emotion from my father, who I'd never seen shed a tear, I answered like the five-year-old boy at the birthday party by nodding my head yes. He said, "What I have right here is a letter I sent your mother five years ago, telling her that I wanted you back home with me."

I held the letter and read halfway down the page, and when I saw, "I WANT MY SON WITH ME," I lost it! I fell in his arms and we both wept. He apologized for not doing more to get me back sooner. It was that "moment" healing began. Fathers and mothers, regardless of the narrative that is shared with your child that may be negative, you can redefine it with love.

I must be honest with you; the healing process wasn't easy. There were remnants of my abuse that poked its head up, but my father never gave up. He was frustrated at times, and my older sisters wanted to knock me out, because I got away with way more than they did but they loved me enough to let me process and get through it, because the truth is, they didn't know why either. Those on the outside looking in may not have all the answers or know the intricate details of what's going on but, what they can do is be present and supportive and trust the process.

Things were coming together. I was back where I belonged, and the feeling of the moment was again congruent with the people who were around me. One day I walked in my homeroom class, and I saw this beautiful dark-haired, freckled-face young girl, Cheltese Shelton, with flowered stretch pants, a button-down shirt and Timberland boots, and immediately, without a doubt, I knew she would be my wife.

I couldn't wait to tell my grandmother, Christina Phillips-Holtsclaw, who was my pastor at the time. I said, "Grandma, she's the one. I'm going to marry her." I tried to convince her to marry us at 18.

She said, "If you can wait two more years, I'll marry you two."

A week before my twentieth birthday we were married. Through many storms, trials and triumphs we are still standing and in love, not on our own but by the grace of God and the help of those who loved us and wanted us to make it. As of this writing, we will be celebrating 20 years of marriage, 23 years together, five children with us, and one in heaven, waiting on us.

My model, my superman, laid down his cape in January 2006. It was with him that I experienced my moment of validation, and it was through him that I experienced my moment of healing. Since his passing there's not a day that goes by that I don't think about him. I often wish that I had more time with him. I was only 25 years old when he passed; this was a time in my life that I really needed my father. When I was younger, his presence was sufficient, but now as a man, husband and father, more than ever, I need his voice; I need his wisdom.

I guess that's why the Bible says it's good to have children in your youth. Not only because you're strong, but also, you'll have a greater chance, with the providence of God, to live longer and be here for those babies you made.

Now that I'm the man, I want to continue the legacy of my father, while creating my own. When I close my eyes, I want my memory and legacy to be recorded as, "He gave more than he asked for," and it is my prayer that my children can say one day, "Daddy made the difference."

7 Things a Child needs from their Father

1. **Respect:** He/She needs to see you love their mother, and if you're not in a relationship with her, at least interact with her respectfully. You are teaching him how to treat women.

2. They need to see you fail well. Own your mistakes, and missteps, and let them see you overcome.

3. **Leadership:** They need to see you lead. You don't have to be Pastor, Mr. CEO, or Mr. President. All you have to be is Dad. That's the only position in your life that can never be filled by anyone else.

4. **Physical presence and Emotional Presence:** They need to see you and feel you. It's ok to cry.

5. **Unconditional Love:** No matter what they do, or where they go, they must know that their father loves them. Your relationship with your children has the ability to enhance their connection with God.

6. **Affirmation:** The words of a father are like jet fuel. They will empower your children to heights unknown.

7. **Support:** They may not take over the family business, they may not be as athletic as you, they may not have interest in anything you have done. But support them, because your children should be an extension of your legacy and have the opportunity to go farther than you without hindrance.

Carlos J. Avent is a higher education professional, a self-published author and a youth/young adult self-development mentor. Carlos was born and raised in Baltimore City, is an alumna of The Baltimore City College, Morgan State University with a B.A. in Sociology, and Walden University with an M.S in Higher Education. His first literary work was self-published in 2018 and is titled, '10 Extraordinary Lessons from an Ordinary Dad' (available on Amazon). It tells the story of his father's wit, mistakes and knowledge that helped him shape his own manhood. Today, Carlos is in his 10th year of marriage to his high school sweetheart, Kellé, and a father to his little princess, Lyric.

HEIR TO THE THRONE:
THE RIGHTFUL PLACE OF FATHERHOOD

CARLOS J. AVENT

. . . .

In order to know where I'm going, you must know where my roots lie. As a father, you are the king of your castle. That is how I saw my father. He commanded respect on his worst day and made you want to listen on any given day. Seeing that in him is what made me want to be like him. I know now, at 36 years old, my fatherhood perspective is rooted not only in the father that I have become, but also rooted in the father that I was privileged to see, grow with and learn from. Like a king passing on the throne to his son, my father's approach to fatherhood is the throne he passed on to me.

I grew up in a two-parent household in the '80s and '90s. That's something that cannot be taken lightly or taken for granted no matter how taboo it sounds to some. I had many friends who didn't grow up with their father present in their lives. For some it was due to an untimely death. For others, it was an absence that felt like death. As a child, I never questioned my friends about it. I just always assumed their father was there unless they told me otherwise. For those who told me they didn't have their father with them, I felt bad for them. I felt like they were missing out, but at the same time, even at an early age, I counted my blessings for having mine in the home with me.

My father was very present. He was fun, he was strict, and he taught me life lessons, both directly and indirectly, every day. I watched how he treated me and my three other siblings so that no one ever felt slighted. I imagine he learned how to balance a multi-children home from his own experience of being one of ten children and watching how his father managed that parental juggling act. He did it well. I always felt like when we talked or spent any time together, it was just us. Never did I feel slighted or as if I lacked.

I struggled to make friends during my early years in school and in the neighborhood. I wasn't outspoken, I didn't have fancy name brand shoes, I wasn't the most athletically gifted, nor was I much of a gamer. I wasn't exactly the kind of kid that other kids gravitated toward. Knowing this made going on field trips in school quite the fun yet anxiety-riddled experience for me. Why? Because the idea of being put into a group and being the outcast in that group was a scary thought to me. That is, unless my father was coming with me. I noticed that whenever my father was around, he was "that dad" that everyone wanted to slap high-fives with and be assigned to his group. This happened all the time, everywhere, not just on school field trips, but more on that later. As an example, if it was a school field trip and my dad volunteered to chaperone, you would see the hands go up in the air swiftly, followed by *"Can I be in Carlos' father's group?"*

This was because my father did something simple that a lot of my peers simply needed. He made them feel welcomed and important.

For some, who may not have had a father figure at home, this was the closest shot they had at experiencing that. Either way, my father was popular. Because he was popular, I made a lot of friends because of the coolness and open-arms congeniality of my father whenever he was around my peers. As I noticed how my father showed love and respect to my peers that made them return that love and respect, it would at times make me think of when it would be my time to chaperone my kid on a field trip. **I knew that this was the type of father I wanted to be.**

As much of a fun guy as my father was in public and around my peers, he was just as much of a fun guy to be around at home. One of my favorite things to do with him at home was to play chess. I started watching him play chess when I was seven years old. He played with guys in the barbershop and occasionally his good friend from his high school days would stop by on Sundays, and they would play chess on the front porch after a Sunday dinner prepared by my mother.

It didn't take long for me to want to know how to play after seeing my father so focused and having fun playing the game. Though the game itself looked boring and slow, what I saw was another thing that I could do with my father, a hobby that he and I would share—something that could be "our thing". So one Sunday after his good buddy left, he brought me to the kitchen table to show me the basics. That first night, he just went over how pieces move and how to win. This became a Sunday thing for us right out of the gate. Through the weeks he would keep showing me the basics, but he also began telling me how the game mirrors life.

Every chess lesson from then became about the game and navigating through life and life choices. He used to talk to me through the game, explaining every move he made and relating it to a real-life scenario. Or he would see that I was about to make a move that didn't make sense or there was a better one to make. He would say, "*Hol'up... look at the whole board boy... you're in danger.*" It was as if he used this time to teach me how to survive when he wasn't around. He was teaching me how to make smart decisions, how to exercise patience, and how to handle losing as a learning opportunity.

These chess lessons at the table lasted for 18 years. As time progressed, I learned more, I got better at the game, but more importantly, I grew from a boy to a man. The way that my father used those opportunities to bond with me, teach me, and mold me, **I knew that this was the type of father that I wanted to be.**

Though my father was home and made his presence felt, he also worked a lot. He needed to care for a home, a family, bills, and all the things that come with being an adult. Between 1997 and 2006, it felt like he was at work more than home. There was always a job for him to go to. I recall spells of time where he would work one job from 7:30am to 4:30pm, then go to the next one from 6:00pm to 10:00pm, and then the last one some late evenings from 11:00pm until he finished the job. That would leave him with maybe three hours of sleep per night on average for about three to four nights per week. Sometimes on Sundays he would sleep until one in the afternoon. Occasionally, I would ask if I could go to work with him, just because I knew that meant I would have a chance to spend time with him, especially as our Sunday chess game time began to dwindle. It didn't matter to me if we were going to the day job at the supermarket where he was the manager of the seafood and deli departments, the part-time evening job where he was a stock and inventory associate, or the overnight job where he cleaned small offices. If I could go, I would have my shoes on without hesitation, not only because it was an opportunity to spend time with my father, but to see him in his element. It was interesting to me to see how he conducted himself at work. In a way, I wanted to see if he would be the way he was when he was being my father or if he changed when at work and became a different type of guy that I had never seen before, if that makes sense.

Watching him at work was like watching your favorite boxer get in the ring or a quarterback take the field. He would just be locked in, doing everything with precision, cutting no corners, and genuinely enjoying what he did. He was also the guy everyone wanted to be around or work with. His work ethic was outstanding and purposeful. As he told me once, "*Whatever you do, you do it with 110%. Doesn't matter if you're the boss or the janitor. You be the best at it and always give your best effort.*" Just like those chess game lessons, this too was a mental note.

Those workdays felt like an eternity sometimes, especially during those times before we had our first family car, but I was fine with it. Those days meant that if I went to work with my father, I needed to get up early enough with him to catch two buses to get to his job. During this era, my father often worked at one of the community supermarkets. The commutes varied. Only once do I recall us being able to walk to his job. For the most part in the early days, it meant that we needed to catch a bus or two to get there. We'd walk to the first bus stop, be on that bus for 20 to 25 minutes, then walk to the second bus stop and be on that bus for maybe another 15 to 20 minutes. No matter what, throughout the entire journey, there seemed to be at least three people in that entire trip that my father would know and have a small conversation with. It felt like he knew everyone, or everyone knew him. Sometimes they would be customers, sometimes old friends that he grew up with or just people he saw on his commute often and developed a kinship with.

What remained consistent in those interactions was how my father included me in the moment. I didn't get to veer off into my own imagination and act invisible. He also wasn't the type of parent who would hush me just because *"grown folks are talking."* He would introduce me, talk about something I was doing or had done, and express how proud of me he was. Sometimes, he would mention something about me to whomever he was speaking to, and I would be amazed at what he said. Not because I didn't want whatever he had said to be made public, but because it was in that moment that I may have realized that my father noticed something about me that I didn't even know he was aware of. It could be a good grade that I got in math class or a drawing I did and had in my drawing book. The fact that he shared it made me feel important and I knew it was genuine and intentional. Seeing my father's intention and pride, I knew two things from that moment forward. First, I never wanted to disappoint him. Second, **I knew that this was the type of father that I wanted to be.**

Fast forward through time; now the crown is placed upon my head and the throne is mine to ascend to.

I became a father in 2009, at the age of 26. Though it was the usual long road, it seemed like it happened overnight to me. Just like that, the days of me searching for a purpose came to a halt and that purpose suddenly became very clear to me. All the years of observing, learning, and taking in the mental notes from my father were about to finally pay off in a big way. It was my time to show him that he did well. It was my time to show him that I was listening and to show him that he provided a great example for me to follow. These were my thoughts from the days leading up to the birth of my first-born love to the moment we all arrived home.

The home that was once a bachelor pad apartment had been transformed into a home for my family. For me, this was a life goal accomplished. It happened just the way I wanted it to happen as well. I just wanted to graduate college and have financial stability before becoming a father. It was important to me to ensure I was able to be a father without any other stressors interfering in the love, time, and attention that I would give to my child. So those two things were already checked off the list. As I got settled in and just looked back at my child, I said to myself, *"I have a daughter."* It was in that moment, that moment of verbalizing it aloud, that it became a reality to me.

I had learned a lot from my father in how he raised me. It just dawned on me that I would have to alter some of the approach because I had a little girl we named Lyric. Why? Well, what's the one thing that connects you to your favorite song that has become the soundtrack of your life, a lyric. Anyway, I felt prepared, but I knew that I was going to have to go with the flow on a few things as well. Being a father to a girl is different. It softens the heart of the man. All the myths and sayings about being a daddy's girl and that girl having her father wrapped around his finger are true indeed. It's different because you innately become overprotective. You're overprotective from everything, not just people. I mean overprotective to the point where if she fell on the floor, it would make me want to dig up the floor, throw it out and put in a new and better one that would treat her right as she crawled around. I imagined if I had a son, and he fell on the floor, we'd just have a talk about how to avoid the floor next time. With a girl, it was totally different.

As I journeyed through the first years of fatherhood, I learned more and more about my personal and newfound depths of compassion, empathy, and love, all of which are rooted in the art of listening. That's right, this little girl taught me to speak less and listen more. Listen to not just the spoken but listen for what goes unspoken. The unspoken moments of just wanting me to be present, to play with her, to watch her play with her toys, to look at her scribbled drawings instead of just saying, "*uh-huh*," and to know when she just needs a hug. These small things were forging a big bond at an early age between my little girl and me. It was reminiscent of how my father was intentional with me.

Sometimes, I think my father had it easy raising me. Not because he had my mother's presence, love and support, but because the world was a bit slower and the digital/information age was not yet in existence. Being an elder statesman of the millennial generation meant that my time to become a parent would pose different challenges and opportunities for me. When I was growing up, my father didn't have to worry about constant media influence by way of technology and social media or worry about the content of what

I was watching or being exposed to due to online end user trends and behaviors. In today's age of parenting, those things must be considered. He didn't have to be concerned with cyberbullying correlating with real-life bullying. I either had different challenges or the same challenges but on steroids 30 years later.

While my father and I had chess to bond over, Lyric and I have our own bond as well. Art. That has become a common place for us. One day I showed her my drawings from when I was young like her, perhaps around eight years old at the earliest. My father wasn't much of an artist himself, but he encouraged me every step of the way with my work. Just like our chess sessions came with life lessons, the art sessions I have with Lyric do as well. Mostly, we discuss patience, trial and error, uniqueness and being proud of your work no matter if it wins first place or is dead last. Overall, this bond for us helps her with her confidence. For me, I turned to art because it was the one talent that I could hang my hat on to make friends and have something that I could do that not everyone else could do. For her, it's a lot like what chess was for me with my father. For Lyric this is OUR thing.

By the time Lyric was school age, I was ready. Remembering the times my father accompanied me on trips, I was looking forward to my opportunity to spend that time with my princess and be the "cool dad." The first time I accompanied Lyric on a field trip with her classmates was to the infamous and timeless Pumpkin Farm, that mid-October classic school field trip. This was an easy one. It's simply touring a farm, getting a pumpkin, taking a hayride, going through a corn maze, eating lunch and going home. What I was most excited about was the chance to be the "cool dad." I remember getting to the classroom, high-fiving kids, asking them how excited they were, and seeing that proud look on Lyric's face—a look I know very well because it was my look when it was my father and I was in school. I got my student assignment of whom I was chaperoning, and it was a mix: Lyric and another girl, and two boys. It was a good day and a successful first run at me being "cool dad."

Fast forward some years: I've conquered the "cool dad" status. Kids high-five me willingly now. I've become 'Mr. Avent'. That was eerie to me because I was so used to my father being 'Mr. Avent' and me just being Carlos, 'Lyric's Dad' or 'Daddy' when it comes to Lyric. But here I was, embracing it all until another conquest stood before me that my father was unable to prepare me for: the infamous first crush.

It was quite harmless, I must say, and flattering to know that my princess was being "the most likable girl in class." However, I took pride in having the opportunity to be the dad that the boys were going to have to deal with. It was my first go-round, so I wanted to do my best. I must say, the boy was impressively confident, unshaken, and ready—all at the age of eight. His name was Derrick. On this day, I dropped Lyric off at school and walked her inside. I was high-fiving her friends because again, I was the cool dad, and Derrick came up to me and got his high-five but was still standing there. Odd, but still there. It appeared he had something to say. So I looked at him and before I could say a word, he dropped the bomb on me.

Derrick: *Mr. Avent... Ima take Lyric to the Valentine's Day dance.*

Me: *Say what?*

Derrick: *Ima take Lyric to the Valentine's Day dance.*

Me: (leaning in a bit closer) ... *One more time, son.*

Derrick: *Ima take Lyric to the Valentine's Day dance.*

Me: *Is that right.* (I looked at Lyric.) ... *do you know him?*

Lyric: *Yes Daddy, that's Derrick!*

Me: (Looked back at the boy) *Derrick, huh.... so, you gonna be her date huh? Is that right?* (Insert Denzel Washington cool laugh)

Me: (fixed my school shirt collar) *Ok... we'll see how that works out.*

Derrick ran off smiling, administrators were smiling and laughing, and I was still processing what had happened in these last three minutes of my fatherhood journey. I thought this wasn't supposed to happen until the prom years. But, that moment of my fatherhood journey, that moment of being respectfully asked for my daughter's company, was an honor—like a prince coming to my castle to request my daughter's hand.

Later that day, I went to pick up Lyric from school and guess who I saw standing with his mother.... that's right, little Derrick.

His mother said he told her he liked Lyric and wanted to ask her to the dance. She said he was blushing at the mention of her name, so she instructed him to first ask me (though he didn't really ask... it was more of an affirmative statement), and she next wanted to meet Lyric and me. Upon leaving, Lyric looked to me and said, "*So I guess he's my boyfriend now.*"

I thought, *Uh. No. But I won't burst your bubble, yet.*

When I look at the relationship between my father and me, and then the subsequent relationship dynamic between my daughter and me, it reminds me of the Lion King and the Lion King 2 stories. If you haven't seen them both, I recommend them. Anyway, my relationship with Dad was a lot like Simba's relationship to Mufasa. Dad was the king of our pride and I just wanted to follow in his footsteps. I wanted to be like him, I wanted to be around him, and I "just couldn't wait to be king."

One distinct difference: Dad wasn't plotted against by his brother with the agenda of taking over his home. Dad is still with us today.

Back to the story.

In Lion King 2, Simba is now a father himself, to a girl cub named Kiara. Simba's initial thoughts on fatherhood were to rule and govern as his father Mufasa did. However, he quickly learned that Kiara was different. She was her own being with her own personality and her own needs. He was extremely overprotective of her, as if he would have her wrapped in a plastic bubble away from all harm if he could. Then as time moved on, Simba learned that although his father's advice was meaningful and useful, he still had to be his own type of father to be the best father he could be for Kiara.

It is a cartoon movie, I know. However, it carries such a unique parallel to my experience and perspective on black fatherhood. My perspective on black fatherhood feels and has always felt like royalty. With it comes a unique responsibility to teach, protect, encourage, and love. The only way to do that is to be present. Physical presence is one thing, but emotional presence is another. As I grew and was taught, protected, encouraged and learned from my father and his presence, I eventually assumed the throne of fatherhood as my own man, prepared to give my best to my princess. **My hope is that she loves the father that I have become as much as I love being her father.**

 **Nathaniel K. Harris, Sr.** is best described as a man of great faith in God. Married with four children, family is the most important thing. Nathaniel has the opportunity to use his gifts in various ways. He is a Full-time employee, Associate Pastor, Musician, Athletic Coach and Mentor. Nathaniel is currently attending Regent University pursuing a Bachelor of Arts degree in Biblical and Theological studies. One of the greatest things Nathaniel has is a wonderful imagination. He enjoys creating opportunities to make those around him smile because of what he says or has done.

THE MISSING BLUEPRINT

NATHANIEL K. HARRIS

• • • • • • • • • • • •

Great architects have the skill to build great monuments and design buildings. This is all done by having the unique ability to read and understand blueprint designs. All details are accurately measured, markers are set, and all edges are accounted for. In other words, blueprints are detailed plans for how something should be made or created. When it comes to building, well-versed persons who are familiar with plans and blueprints can successfully build anything.

When I think of a master builder, I can consider my grandfather. Grason Harris, Jr. was considered the greatest builder of his time. Born 1916, my grandfather was raised in an era when most African Americans were not afforded the privilege of a quality education. Everything that he ever learned was hands-on and by experience. He had many skill sets, but most notable was his ability to build houses from the ground up. When he passed away in 2018, he was 102 years of age. His claim to fame was that he was able to build houses with just a tape measure but never a blueprint. He had a keen eye to make markings and measure cuts to the exact measurement. Building was natural for him.

Most of my uncles were record-setting athletes and awesome leaders. It is my understanding that my grandfather never attended any of their sporting events. He never witnessed their great accomplishments and winning achievements. There was never a time that my grandfather was considered a bad father; he was a provider. The issue, was this a learned pattern or something that men, especially Harris men, would do?

My father, Richard Harris, has been a pillar when it comes to striving to be a better father. Growing up, my father did the best that he could when it came to providing, being a father and being a husband. One of the things that was a constant is that we were in church Wednesday through Sunday. We were a family of musicians, so we were to be in service to aid in ministry. Our grades were below standard, we were tired most of the time; however, we all still graduated from high school. After we were well into our adulthood, my dad would apologize for the way we were brought up. Some may have thought his methods were unorthodox or selfish. All I recall him saying is that he only did what he knew to do.

There was a time in my adult life that I needed my dad badly. After I went through my divorce in 2004, I hit an all-time low spot in my life. I had been married; it was supposed to be a forever deal. It appeared that everything was being taken from me. I lost family, cars and material things after I could not afford to make payments. My dad was gracious enough to pick me up in the mornings to take me to work. Often, he would pick me up from work and then bring me back home. Many mornings I would ask questions to just get some answers concerning what I was going through. I remember asking Dad, "What did we ever do wrong?"

I remember my dad responding in his own way, "Let me know when you find out." From that point on I had a new respect for him as my father. I listened to him share things about his marriages that I did not know. Married three (3) times, he was able to offer some awesome testimony regarding his perspective on being a black man. He shared that he didn't necessarily have a great example of a blueprint of being a father or a husband. The only thing he knew, and saw was hard work and just making it happen. When the church became a part of his life, the lesson he learned was having faith in God and being faithful to ministry.

Unfortunately, there was a pattern that was passed down from my grandfather. My dad did not attend too many of our sporting events. When my brother and I were active in sports programs, the greatest thing would have been to see my dad in the stands cheering us on. My mother was not around us at the time; however, my father was doing the best that he could to raise two growing teenagers. Although my dad may not have been to many of our athletic events, he was there when I absolutely needed him.

One of the greatest rewards of being an adult is the ability to fall in love, marry, create and raise children. When a couple falls in love, one of the rewards of the union is the birthing of children and the anticipation of what they will become. In the anticipation of the children's success, we often forget about the care and maintenance of the relationship. Some relationships thrive through adversities;

however, there are those that seem to implode due to lack of care and maintenance. Behind the unfortunate events of some failed relationships, there are children.

After I was remarried to my second wife, I realized that I wanted and needed to do something different. I did not believe that I could go into this marriage as I did the first one. I also had to understand that I could not carry the pain of the first marriage into this one. The fact that I married my friend was important. We were able to discuss everything, and we made sure communication was an essential part of our relationship. We found out that we were going to need to keep our family business to ourselves and we needed to keep other family members out. The object of the husband and wife was to be fortified and to not allow other people to interfere with the growth of their marriage. When we began to have children of our own, I had to parent differently than I did before.

When raising children from other people, the assignment is to love them all the same. It would appear that the younger children would get more attention and more gifts than the older children. This also could suggest that the older children received less love and affection. One of the things that I had to do as a father was to ensure that my oldest children were given the same amount of attention and the same amount of love as my youngest children. The overwhelming issue was my oldest children lived in another state approximately four hours away. It was difficult to get to them and difficult to make the adjustments to spend time with them. Unfortunately, I had to love long distance. Although I was still paying child support, there was no communication about visitation and our time together was gradually becoming minimal.

Around three years ago, I was able to obtain primary custody of my oldest son. My oldest daughter is now an adult and is working to be a great adult woman. The learning curve that I am experiencing now is learning to parent a teenager. Some may not understand this, so let me explain. My children and I were separated through divorce and their mother was awarded primary custody. I was not able to be a part of their growing experiences and was not afforded the opportunity to revel in the memories of their childhood.

When my oldest son came to live with me, we had to infuse his life with what we already were involved in. My family was already involved in church activities and sports. My wife and I were coaching in the Christian Youth Athletic League and we had our younger sons actively involved. Our schedule was consumed with working full time jobs during the week, sports practice during the week, mid-week ministry meetings, games on Saturday and church services on Sunday. When my oldest son began to get involved with activities for school and work, my wife and I had to alter some plans to make sure that we attended the events that our son was involved in.

Discipline was and is tough for me to deal with. My youngest sons are easier for my wife and me because we have been consistent with discipline since they were young enough to get into mischief. There were times when physical discipline was necessary, and there were times when a stern talking to or a lingering look solved the problem. With my oldest, discipline was a little more interesting. By the time he moved in with me and my wife, he was fifteen years old. As parents, we allowed a little space and time for him to feel his way through this change and the new way of living. There were times that I wanted to emphasize that I was the father; I was in charge. There was a point when I wanted to react to my son as my dad would have and his dad would have. I understood that a good, old-fashioned beating was the way to prove the power of a man to his son.

I remember calling my mom asking for wise counsel. I was inquiring about a suitable way to deal with my growing teenager. My mother suggested something totally different than I would have expected. My mom suggested that I do something different from the norm. The question was what was the norm? I know to body slam and throw punches. I know to yell and scream. I know to violently react. I know to lose all control until you start seeing white stars. The one thing that I needed to do was to be a good father during one of the most difficult times and learning stages of his young life. What he didn't need was an angry father. What he didn't need was a tyrant. What was effective, and still is, is having a dad who was patient and willing to communicate when tough times were certain.

As mentioned, I had never seen this age in parenting. My wife and I had been parenting our youngest son together since birth. We had the opportunity to watch the various stages of his development. I was able to witness some of my oldest daughter growing up as a young girl. When my first wife relocated to another state, my daughter was four years old and my oldest son was eight months old. The only thing that I was able to witness was the crawling phase, the cute mumbling and the diaper changing. Other than the baby stage, I was only minimally involved in raising my oldest son.

As a parent, I have made it a mandate that I do all I can to never miss any of my children's events. When it comes to sports, my wife and I are heavily involved in our sons' athletics. We make sure to schedule our engagements around their sports activities. As a bonus, my wife and I both coach in the Athletic League. Over the years, we have witnessed the athleticism of our children. They have been involved with soccer, baseball/t-ball and basketball. When my oldest son became interested in sports and band activities, we had to add to and adjust our already hectic schedule to ensure that he was included.

As mentioned, communication is essential. With everyone having commitments, we all had to be on the same page. We would have weekly table talks to just make sure that our schedules were airtight, no schedule was missed, practices and games were attended, and nothing was omitted. There were times when some engagements were not shared, and we were not able to attend. My oldest son was involved in some high school band performances and the rest of the family could not attend because we already made our plans for the week and there was no communication about any events until the last minute. With transportation, I always wanted to make sure that my children arrived safely. I had no problems or issues with showing up to make sure that my children were picked up and arrived at their destination safely and on time.

When the communication between us failed, my oldest son was responsible for securing his own transportation, either from mass transit or a friend. The point that we were making was we wanted to be there to support him at the events, but we were never told of the event or the time conflicted with something that we already had scheduled. As a father, I am and have always been proud of all my children's accomplishments. We have a makeshift trophy case with the awards from the sports that our sons participated in. The greatest thing is I was there for all the events and I can add the memories that were associated with the trophies.

As a father, I was there for my sons. I made every attempt to be a part of my sons' lives. I am disproving the vicious cycle that black and brown men cannot be in the daily lives of their children. The proud moment is when your children view you as an inspiration and they allow your input and experience to help them in their events. With me being athletic, I enjoy watching my sons excel in various sports. As an admission, my sons are more skilled at their ages than I was. Musically, my oldest son is a better musician than I was at his age. I am proud watching them mature and becoming the men that God has called them to be.

What I discovered through my years of parenting is that trends needed to be destroyed. My dad followed the path of his father, which continued the unfortunate relationship between father and children. I never wanted to be the father who never was involved with the activities of my children. If anything, I am too active, and I am my children's biggest cheerleader. I am the loudest one screaming, and my wife and I are the parents yelling at the officials when the calls are terrible and don't go our team's way. There is a quote from Neil Wood to the effect that we should not get so busy in our careers that we forget to have a life. You can do both. You can make lots of money, become a millionaire AND enjoy time with family, friends AND be a great role model as a parent.

I am so glad that I am a Christian man and believe in governing my family with biblical principles. I believe that the foundation of a family must be grounded and centered on moral ideas that honor and glorify God. The book of wisdom (Proverbs 20:7, New Living Translation) states, "The righteous who walks in his integrity and Godly principles, how blessed are his children after him who have his example to follow." As a Christian father, I have the responsibility of parenting my children with balance. Although I have to commit to the ministry that we are actively involved in, I am also required to be the best representation of God in my home. In other words, I must lead by example. If I tell my children that I will be there and will do something, I must do all I can to make it happen and be a man of my word.

I never want my children to say that I was never there and never supported them. My daughter is living in another state and is doing well. I recently had the opportunity to be the father that my daughter needed. She cried out for help when she was trying to navigate through life's issues. She was able to come visit for a few weeks to retreat and heal her mind, body and spirit from what she was going through. My sons are all together. My oldest is in his senior year of high school. My younger sons are in a joint elementary and middle school studying and working hard.

I do believe that my younger sons are watching to see how I handle my relationship with my oldest son. What they do not hear is a bunch of yelling and cursing. What they continue to hear is communication and people sharing their thoughts, dreams and ambitions. My job as a father is to raise these boys to be great men in God. The job I have is to prepare them for the real world and how to navigate through it.

My oldest son just shared with me that he wanted to be independent and gain "grown-man" status. I had to ask him what that meant. He believed that "grown-man" status was being independent and living on his own. I had to encourage him that that was just a stage of "grown-man" status. This status is achieved when you no longer make selfish decisions. As a man, every decision must include all parties and not cause harm. "Grown-man" status leads you to be responsible for your actions and to make righteous decisions. "Grown-man" status leads you to create a blueprint for being a great father. It leads you to create a blueprint for being a great provider. It leads you to create a blueprint on how to overcome obstacles. It leads you to create a blueprint on how to be a role model to black boys as they grow into men. A blueprint is designed to have a plan to erect a wonderful structure. In terms of a wonderful structure, I am referring to the building of a great structure which is a strong black man committed to loving and caring for his home.

As a father, you are not just a provider but also a protector. My daughter was the first child and the child I was most concerned about. As a young man, I was carefree and reckless. My friends and I were acting like typical single men with no responsibilities. I remember hearing a faint voice telling me, "You will reap what you sow." At the time, I wasn't concerned about a "God-conscience;" my friends and I were only interested in doing what single, reckless men do and think of.

As my life settled and I became more responsible, I wanted to settle down and possibly have children. Lo and behold, my first child was my baby girl. Everything that I longed for and desired was exactly what I prayed against for my daughter. Every little boy who came around her, I was like the big guard dog that would not let anyone come close. There was no way that I would allow anyone to come remotely close to my daughter.

That little girl became a growing young lady. Over the years of our being separated, her attitude changed, her desires changed, and her life started changing and I was not able to be a part of it. There were years of holiday and seasonal visits where I would see both of my oldest children; however, when they got older, the visits became fewer, and unwanted. I was not a part of anything that my daughter was involved with since she was living out of state. I was not able to warn her about reckless men; I could not explain the man's way of thinking.

When my daughter was older, she began to date, and she started making decisions that a young woman would make. She made the choice to move away to be with a man I didn't know, and I was unsure if he could care for her. For the last four years, I've only seen her a few times. Life caused everyone to be busy and we scheduled visits by vacation. There were trips that we had to make to Tennessee and once the business was finished, we would stop in just to do a check to see how she was doing. There were a couple times that my daughter would travel to visit just to get away and to retreat from the normal hustle and bustle of her life. When all is said and done, my daughter is doing well, and I couldn't be prouder.

Known from singing in Motown records R&B group Prophet Jones, **Clarence "KD" McNair** returns to the spotlight as a best-selling author of ' Give It One More Try", dedicated to all the over-comers in the world. McNair shifts his reader's mind from that one negative thought seeking to alter one's life. He shares the different experiences he encountered while working as a national recording artist, and how he improved from his anxiety disor-ders after losing his record label deal for his second album in 2002. For years, McNair suffered greatly from panic attacks and other difficulties. The book shares his road to recovery, and how changing his perspective led to a restored way of living. McNair has traveled many roads however, the most rewarding road has been family, because he gets to use his experiences, good or bad, to help lead his kids in the right direction, hoping they will learn from all the mistakes that he's made in life and will understand that we are never in control of anything, God is, and patience is a virtue. It's better to listen than learn things the hard way. God has blessed Clarence with his son Khori, his daughter Amaria, and his youngest son Marley. McNair states, "My oldest son got straight A's in school and I got chills of joy to know that he will be the better version of me and get to live his youth out, something that I never had a chance to do! My daughter is my sunshine her smile melts my heart. My youngest son, I believe is God's way of giving me another chance. Life is a gift and we must be grateful at all times."

PASSING THE TORCH

CLARENCE KD MCNAIR

* * * * * * * * * * * * *

The torch you pass will determine the legacy that lights forever.

If I were an Olympic runner my torch would be called Dad. All I ever wanted to do was pass the torch—not just any torch, but a torch carried with integrity, dignity, pride, confidence, humbleness, love, and a heart that fears God. All of this, I hope my kids see in my last name, so as the name continues to multiply generation after generation. It's not just a last name, but it stands for something deeper. Some see it as just a last name, but I see it as a reflection of the journey that I experienced in my life. It's what made me who I am today, a proud father, a.k.a. dad. Reflecting over my life, this journey has not been easy. So many ups and downs and different challenges threw me in many directions, like being in the middle of a thunderstorm or tornado.

For a lot of us men life has been one big challenge over and over again. For so many years I would just ask God, "Why me? Why did my life go in a direction that I had no roadmap to understand where I was going?" Growing up in Baltimore, Maryland, in the inner city was not easy, but what took the cake was seeing how Life had played an unfair card to my father, a man who wanted nothing but to help his mother get out of the projects. Unfortunately, it never happened, and my father ended up going to jail, and that was the end of any physical contact with him for a long time. That was my introduction to manhood, before I was even a man. Left unprotected with no direction at all, for years I battled a quiet war within my mind.

My sister, mother and I would take the bus to visit my father from time to time when we were little, and I remember the smile on his face when he saw us come to visit. There were still so many questions racing through my young mind. I would always say to myself, *What am I going to do now? I don't think my dad will ever come back. Why did he go to jail? Was he just being a bad person? Why is my dad a bad person? What did he do for everybody to know he's a bad person?* As I got older and I became an adult I realized my dad was not a bad person. Like many of us, my dad was misunderstood. He was a man with a heart of gold, with limited resources, who always had good intentions but went about them the wrong way.

You see, the most valuable things in life are free; however, so many had their freedom taken from them because the torch that was handed down to them was lack, poverty, fear, worry, anxiety, doubt, a very restricted life, brokenness, and no directions. Everything in life has a beginning; no one asked to come into this world on the negative side of the track. However, the reality of it all is, you have the haves and the have-nots, leaving lots of men to fend for themselves and find a way to make a come-up, even if it's not the best way. When you live a minimum life most of the time you reach for the closest things around you! And we all know growing up in the inner cities there aren't many resources around, except for the ones that always end up taking your freedom. Not because there is no hope or other ways to get it; sometimes you just show the characteristics of the torch that has been handed down to you.

As a father I always battled day to day, wondering if I was doing enough for my kids; if they saw all that I tried to do; if they felt the love I tried my best to give; if they saw me trying to give them something to carry throughout their lives. To the rest of the world it may look and sound easy but being a black dad is far from an easy job, especially when you did not get any head-start help! You had to start from ground zero. So I want people reading this book to understand that things that may look easy for some are a breakthrough for others. A lot of us did not have everything but we were willing to do the work needed to fix whatever needed to be changed and focus on things that would help us grow in ways that no one ever believed was possible. All because you made a difference, to make sure that your kids will not have to deal with the same thing you did, especially if you grew up like most men in my community, without their father, leaving the house off balance.

Most people see the world as full of opportunity, but for some of us, sometimes even the opportunities have limits. In my book *Give it One More Try*, I talked about how sometimes you need bricks on your back to tap into your supernatural strength. Sons and daughters, there have been many supernatural nights you just did not know what dad had to deal with, because when you're a man you're not supposed to smile, you're not supposed to cry, you're not supposed to be sad; you're not supposed to not be able to take care of your family. So when things were rough not only was the stress high, the thoughts ran high wondering how everyone would view you in your rough times.

Through the eyes of a father we sometimes feel that after all we do right, everyone is still waiting for a fall. So when we do prove everyone wrong and get back up and give it one more try the first thing we do is look for approval and that really is incredibly stressful. All we want is to love family and unfortunately there are many things that block that free right of fatherhood to have a relationship with your kids. Even if you're not in the best financial space, no man should be kicked out of love. My point is, it takes a village to raise a man and unfortunately a lot of us were left alone to raise ourselves, then the cycle repeats itself time and time again. Thank God for prayer. So many of us have been given a second chance, because we never asked for what came with being born in this world. We did not pick the home that we would live in or the families we were born into that were out of our control. And because of that we had to work so much harder to achieve something more than normal. It's not about feeling sorry for us; it's about understanding us and seeing how being a father is a major step for many of us.

I want to end this by saying I may not be perfect, I may not have it all together, but one thing I have is my title of "dad". No matter what, I will be the best dad I can be because this department of my life matters the most to me. I am willing to do whatever it takes to make sure the torch I pass to my kids represents the best that I can be.

"Words have an awesome impact. The impression made by a father's voice can set in motion an entire trend of life."

Gordon MacDonald

Wiafe Busia, B.Sc is a Sr. Financial Analyst with GE Capital – Atlanta, GA. He is a part-time, proud, single Dad.

Mr. Busia studied in Oslo, Norway, Scandinavia. He lived in Toronto, Canada for many years. He also lived in and traveled to Europe in his late teens. Mr. Busia loves traveling and meeting people from all cultures, especially if they can cook their native cuisine. He loves to cook and try different foods globally. Wiafe is just a plain citizen of the world who loves everyone and appreciates what God has made that we enjoy today and every day.

THROUGH MY LENS

WIAFE BUSIA

• • • • • • • • • • • • •

As an African, born and raised in Ghana Western Africa, being a black father is a privilege and an awesome responsibility that I take very seriously. It's rooted and widely believed in our tradition that society judges you by who your children become in their adult lives, and the status quo kind of compels you to do your fatherly duty with some sense of pride; in other words being called "Dad" is a crown that you look forward to and want to wear for the rest of your life. Of course the environment in which children are raised in their formative years is crucial and a defining period in shaping their lives, meaning that one must make a conscious decision every day to predict the outcome of tomorrow based on the things you do today. This is a model that I have lived up to all my life.

Ernest Hemingway once wrote (famously quoted by President Barack Obama when he eulogized Senator John McCain),

"Today is only one day in all the days that will ever be. But what will happen in all the other days that ever come can depend on what you do today."

I knew then and I still do that my daughter's success in all the other days and years to follow depended on the choices I made from the day she was born.

My daughter was born some 25 years ago, Father's Day 2020, so you can imagine how special that day was for me. She was named after my oldest sister whom I have always looked up to as a mother figure, partly because my sister was 17 years older than me and I spent my first grade year living with her because I wanted to, according to my folks... She had just finished the university and was serving her mandatory one-year national service in another region in Ghana.

My life completely changed after my daughter was born. I grew up instantly, though I was 29 years old. I'd become a "Dad" and I got the baton - the responsibility that I talked about at the beginning, the joy and so many things that were going through my head, all the to-do lists, the playground times, the stroll with her by my side... I was thinking of her in her car seat, out with me to drive and chat, visiting her aunt (my sister) who was living in the same city as us in Canada, just about an hour's drive away, thinking about holding her firmly to my chest when out in malls shopping for toys—heck, I even thought about whipping her butt when she misbehaved and giving her a timeout. All that and even more went through my head in that few seconds as I held her in my arms waiting for her mother to be cleaned up in the OR, then they came for my baby to be cleaned also.

All that is to say that I was proud and I recognized the light suddenly became brighter than it had ever been and I wore that crown of "Dad" that day and am still wearing it because once you're crowned a king you're always a king, figuratively. I was simply ready to walk the walk with my title. I became sensitive with my environment, a compassionate person; all of a sudden, little things that never worried me became concerning to me, and I guess all that was my transitional period which I took very seriously. I knew I was the pivotal figure in my daughter's life and would shape her to what I'd like to see in her as an adult. A year later we celebrated her first birthday and she was the joy of my heart, watching her running around. A child's birthday turned into an adult's party, and before we knew it, it was 4am, kids were all asleep, and dads and moms were shaking it on the dance floor like never before—fun days!

Unfortunately, things sometimes don't always turn out as planned or thought of in a perfect world. My relationship with my now ex ended soon after our daughter turned one year. We separated and I accepted a job offer and moved to the United States. My daughter and her mother stayed in Canada.

Our separation and eventual divorce did not stop me from loving my daughter. The key factor in all that was transpiring at the time was my LOVE for my baby, and truth be told, I still extended that love to my ex over the years. It was never easy to work things from a distance, but I made every effort to be there for my little girl.

From the very beginning her mother and I agreed that it wasn't about the two of us (parents) but rather everything was about that little one. We worked out the financial aspect of caring for our baby, which became my number one priority in my day-to-day life. I was on the phone with my daughter every day to see her growing; we even did some homework together over the phone. I would fly over to see some of her recitals as convenient. I visited more than four times a year to Canada to see her and spend time with her. The verbal agreement with my ex was that she would spend every summer and every other Christmas with me in the United States, and she did. We'd travel for summer holidays together with the lady I was dating at the time. It was important for me to let anyone that came into "our" life know that my daughter was my everything, so the smart women knew exactly how to play it and frankly, it worked out just fine. We would travel to Disney every other year or so, a couple of times just my baby and me for a weeklong vacation. My preferred means of traveling was to drive, and she loved it.

Going on vacation, I chose to drive for the most part if the distance was less than seven hours. Sometimes we'd plan to stay overnight on the way in a city that seemed fun and interesting because we'd be alone for several hours driving. To me it was my bonding time but to her it was a road trip. After she spent every summer vacation with me, I'd drive her back to Canada for the new school year and meet her new teachers and chat with the prior year's teachers as well. This continued throughout her elementary, middle and high school years. We traveled to many places; that, to me, was part of me helping shape her views of the world that she was growing into and appreciating the world as it was and all that it had to offer.

From the day she was born, I never stopped loving and being there for her and I realized that from my own culture and tradition that what my baby would become as an adult depended on how I helped shape her into that future, knowing that my priorities were straight and determined to make it work every minute.

The bigger piece of all these, the unsung hero, is her mother, with whom communication wasn't the greatest but respectable. Sometimes that's all we need to work through any differences. I used the word respectable because it shouldn't take kisses to understand that a child needs love and perspectives from both parents to thrive and succeed in life. Her mother and I had differences, our friends might say a lot of misunderstandings, sometimes just hearsay through mutual friends of misconstrued conversations that happened prior, but no matter what our differences, we always understood that it was about our baby and not us.

My mindset was that she was my legacy and what I did, my attitude toward everything I did, would have an impact on her and would shape her life forever. We went through the same routine year after year and on to college away from home, about six hours' drive from home. I would visit her at college, several times, and stayed for weekends. During this visit we would do road trips to nearby cities for a night; she loved the road trips. This was regular till she graduated from college and moved back home with her mother again, though I thought she was going to move in with me, but that was just wishful thinking.

At almost 25 years old now, she's still my baby and I'm her Dad; that connection is the foundation that I laid from the day she was born. What I think made it easier for me was that I took a different approach with my ex, that communication was the only way to give our baby our best and that all personal feelings should be kept aside. That's not to say we never had an issue or differences, but we managed to not allow it to trickle down on our baby, and that is very imperative that every couple, in or out of relationship, should understand.

I believe the larger percentage of fathers would want to be there for their children but many of them at times lack communication between them and their exes, which disables the child's ability to see and receive the affection they deserve; in the interim it becomes easier for men to give up to avoid regular confrontations. Every child needs both parents in their life one way or another. Folks don't need to be together as wife and husband to parent their child, but they must have a good working communication.

Fathers are a huge part of any kid's life. It is common to see family separations end up with kids spending most of the time with their mothers, but I do believe and I'm not alone, that the majority of fathers love to spend time also with their kids. Financially it can be hard for some, but then again, good working communication can bridge that gap. I knew from the beginning that I didn't have to be financially well off in order to take care of my responsibility to my child and when I didn't have the means at any given time when the need was very desperate, I would communicate way ahead to my ex—the same with when things were good on my end; I would extend extra.

While I do realize that every situation is different, there is one thing that must remain consistent: making your words matter to the child, keeping your promises and surprising the child sometimes. Almost every vacation we went on she would want to buy her mother a gift and I'd pay for it. Those things create memories they always will remember, and it only fosters the relationship for a better trajectory.

Above all, I learned to give my ex a kind of respect that I can only display toward my boss at work who gives me all the work and extra work... if you know what I mean. We have all heard the common phrase that respect is earned—true! But I also think that respect could be given in a circumstance that will make peace reign for the greater good, and that was a component of my working communication with my ex. I never argued with my ex in my daughter's presence or complained about my ex to my daughter. I'd like to think that I have the largest ego in the whole wide world and I know that it's hard for anyone to break through our egoistic mind frame, which most men do have, but the truth is women do have egos too. Theirs are much softer but HARDER to break through if fellas are not real with themselves.

In all, my daughter meant everything to me from the day she was born, and I guess that meant I would love her forever. Throughout the years, I thought of myself as being the only role model she'd know and the only one she should ever know. It meant a lot more to me than anything else that I was and still am there for her. I looked forward to seeing her at every opportunity that I got, and I still do; not being at home together with her mother did not stop me from being a dad, and it did not stop me from making sure that she had a dad, too, just like every child deserves.

No matter what uncompromising situations may come my way, I never unloaded them on her; she has always been shown nothing but love. And now anytime I see her, I take a second look at her— how quickly she's become a grown young woman. Sometimes I dive into a few seconds of reminiscing over the past 25 years with her, but what warms my heart now, really, is I see exactly what I envisioned of her more than two decades ago. She's a smart and caring, hardworking young lady, very much informed and ready to make her own mistakes in order to succeed.

You see, fatherhood is not just to father a child; rather, it is a mental journey that one must be ready and willing to take. It's a physical, mental, emotional and financial journey, with plenty of happiness and joyous moments, that has its ups and downs along the way, but giving up because of hard times or disagreements between the parents should never be an option. A lot of sacrifices and better working communication is a big part of making it work. Most men equate fatherhood to finances, which does have a huge basis to it but that's not all there is to it; providing financially or making child support payments on time and every month does not complete one's fatherhood. My idea of fatherhood was to be physically present at all costs, besides the financial responsibilities and as often as I could, and the most important thing of all to me was not breaking a promise. I always spoke to her looking into her eyes, so she understood me and believed in me.

My only appeal to our women is that you please allow fathers in, when they are willing to be there physically and not only when they're paying the money... even when there's no money coming in; still let them be the father if they're willing and want to be. Separate or channel your grievances differently and don't lump it into one. The father may be financially irresponsible but please do not deny the child the chance to know their father, even in the worst situations. It is part of their formative years, so they learn of the right decisions and choices to make. In reality, more often than not, the clues were there from the beginning when you all met and before they were born.

"A good father is one of the most unsung, unpraised, unnoticed, and yet one of the most valuable assets in our society."

Billy Graham

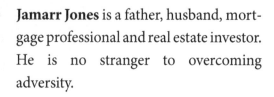

Jamarr Jones is a father, husband, mortgage professional and real estate investor. He is no stranger to overcoming adversity.

Growing up in Baltimore, Maryland, he began his journey into manhood with becoming a father of twin girls at the age of eighteen.

The challenges and influences from his environment became stronger over time and he began making wrong decisions. Jamarr was incarcerated multiple times as a young adult. Amid these make or break life experiences he rededicated his life to God. He started sharing the Word and encouraging others who were also incarcerated to do the same.

While incarcerated Jamarr spent much of his time writing Gospel Rap. He wanted to come home and stand for positivity. Upon his release he was able to take all that he had written and start "Jamarr Rashan Making Hits for the Lord". Exposing his Gospel Rap talents throughout the DMV, in churches, through community outreach, graduations and events, his music has led many people to grow closer to God and has inspired them to live a more positive lifestyle.

As a mortgage and real estate investment professional, with almost fifteen years' experience, Jamarr takes pride in helping his clients through the process from start to finish; whether through education, loan assistance or guiding them to their best financial situation.

It has been a long journey, however, Jamarr currently shares his story from struggle to success to many who have lost hope and need motivation.

TRULY A GIRL DAD

JAMARR JONES

• • • • • • • • • • • • •

Jamarr Rashan Jones is the father of four dynamic young ladies, each unique and special in her individual way.

I think back on the day 19 years ago, walking into Harbor Hospital with my high school girlfriend, after just a few days earlier breaking the toughest news to my mother in my 17 years of life on this planet. At the time leading up to the conversation I was literally scared because I did not know how she would react to the news. This was something that could shift our relationship for life. She could possibly disown me, put me out of her house or go upside my head. These were some of the thoughts that were running their own little track meet in my mind. I was convinced that these were all very possible reactions to the information that I had to share with her.

At this time in my life I was 17 years old and had just started my senior year in high school. I was a decent student; I was on the work-study program since the second half of my junior year. My routine was going to school in the morning. I took two classes and was out by 10:30 am. I didn't have a car, but I did ride my dirt bike to school and to work to my full-time job at Sylvan Prometrics. I was making $9.50 an hour and minimum wage was $5.15 an hour, so to be 17 and have a full-time job, I was doing pretty well for myself. I was also a shooting guard on my high school championship basketball team, looking to defend our Baltimore county championship my senior year. I never got into any major trouble, so I think that my parents considered me at this time a good son, a good role model for my younger brother and was on the road to college.

I can't remember the room that we were in but with a serious look and an equally very nervous voice, I told my mother and my step-father that we had to talk. The look that I had on my face instantly triggered concern in both of their eyes. I took a deep breath and proceeded to tell them my girlfriend was pregnant. A look of dis-belief, a scream of, "Oh Jamarr," and even worse than the racing thoughts in my mind, a look of total disappointment and heart-break. She started crying and yelling. I made my mother cry, the woman who sacrificed so much for me and my little brother to have a decent life. I would have rather she had gone upside my head.

After a few days of the news that I was having a baby with the next-door neighbor started spreading around, and my mother's blood pressure started going down, I was at the hospital meeting the radiologist that was performing the checkup and, little did I know, the ultrasound. A nice lady, Caucasian, about 50-something, was taking us through the first visit process. My girlfriend was on the table and the lady had gel and a device rubbing it on her stomach, trying to find a heartbeat. She then said, "I found the heartbeat." So we listened to the heartbeat for about 30 seconds. It was a happy moment. Then, when I thought the process was over, she then stated in a joking way, "I think I hear something over here." She applied more gel and rubbed the device over the opposite end of her stomach and then said, "I just found another heartbeat." I didn't understand what was going on but they both were laughing and celebrating. She then told me that there was another baby. I still didn't get it. She spoke slowly and said it was twins, two babies. I was struck speechless and all I could think about was I had just broken the news about one baby but now I had to explain that we were having twins. This was where my journey through fatherhood began, seventeen years old, a high school senior, living in my mother's house, becoming the father of not one but two of God's most precious gifts.

I'm proud and blessed to have been a part of their growth and development. Here's a little about what each one of these young ladies is currently doing.

Jade

Jade is 19 years old and an excellent student, a freshman at Morgan State University, and is currently on a full scholarship. She was recently honored at a banquet because she maintains a 4.0 GPA and just received an award right before the school's shutdown due to Covid-19. She maintains a part-time job and is currently majoring in theatre and doing excellent.

When Jade was born, she was the first to enter the world, seven minutes before her twin sister. With all of the uncertainty of me being a new father at the age of seventeen and being the father of twin girls, when I saw Jade's beautiful, precious face, the love that I felt let me know that whatever was needed for me to be an effective father, I would do. I knew at that very moment that I had everything that I needed to be the pillar of strength, the loving and supportive father that she would need.

What most people don't know is when you have twins and they are the same gender you have to come up with a strategy on the names. During our doctors' visits each baby was known as Baby A and Baby B. We agreed that when the first baby was born, her name would be Jade, and the second baby would be Jewel. I was blessed to have a healthy baby girl who needed my love and support.

Having twins and seeing how they fought for their own identity was interesting. We always dressed Jade in the color pink and Jewel in the color purple. But they always had their own distinct personalities. Jade loved to have fun but was also reserved like me. It's funny what we can pass through genetics; some of the facial expressions that Jade makes are the exact same ones that I make to this day. She has impressed me over the years with her conviction. She will move a mountain to accomplish her goals or fight for what she believes in. I have seen her will herself to victory many times, whether it's graduating with honors in the advanced curriculum at Poly Tech or winning a state championship as a distance runner.

I can remember when she first entered the Baltimore Leadership School for Young Women, which is a Charter School in Baltimore, Maryland, in the sixth grade. I encouraged her and her sister to join the rowing team. I always wanted to expose them to new and different opportunities, to challenge them and for them to have different experiences, because you never know what they might decide to gravitate to. I knew that this was a unique opportunity for them to participate in something that was generally only available in more affluent communities. Well, Jade and Jewel were totally against the idea and decided to participate in other after-school activities. I knew it would also give them the opportunity for an easier path to a scholarship to an Ivy League school. There are scholarships available specifically for minorities in this sport because of the lack of minorities in the sport. I worked hard to convince them for years to give it a shot.

Finally, I was able to get Jade to consider it and go to a tryout when she was in the eighth grade. We went to the boathouse, and this was her first time seeing large canoes, row coaches and teenagers from different schools working out for this sport. She was nervous and wanted to leave. I said that I would be with her every step of the way. I walked her in and stayed while she started her tryout. She made the team and enjoyed being a part of the Baltimore Row Club.

A few weeks later they had to pass a swim test in order to participate in the actual races, even though they wore life jackets while in the water. Now I wasn't aware of the date of the swim test; this was something that they did while in practice. I knew for a fact that at that time my baby girl was not a proficient swimmer. As much as I tried to teach my girls how to swim, she was still getting on my back in anything deeper than four feet. So when I picked her up from practice and she informed me that they had a swim test today, I was expecting that she'd failed the swim test and we needed to get her some swim lessons immediately. She then said that she participated in the swim test; she had to swim back and forth in 10 feet several times and tread water for two minutes. She passed the swim test on the first try. I was shocked and amazed. I asked her how she was able to get over her fear and how she was able to do it. She told me, "Daddy, I really wanted to be able to be a part of their first boat race the following Saturday."

She knew she had to do it in order to race so she just did it. This reflects how Jade has been successful and overcome all challenges.

It doesn't surprise me that Jade is excelling at Morgan State and has clear goals to finish as valedictorian.

Jewel

Jewel is 19 years old and is a freshman at Benedict College in South Carolina. She is currently on a full scholarship. She has a 3.25 GPA. She is majoring in early childhood development and does her internship at the elementary school around the corner from the college. As she recently informed me, Benedict won an award for being the best HBCU in 2018 -2019. She is also a part of the traveling school choir. She surprised me with the choir; I didn't know she had an interest, but she loves the experience.

Even though Jewel came out seven minutes after her twin sister, she has always been willing to let you know that she and her sister were the same age and born on the same day. My fashionista baby girl, Jewel has a beautiful smile and an infectious laugh that will make you laugh once she starts. It's like someone is tickling her all the time. She also feels like she is the boss and that the world just can't handle her. I love her outlook on life. She feels like anything that she wants to do, she can accomplish it and do a great job.

When she was young, she would help take care of her sisters. She loved to cook at an early age and give her sisters instructions on cleaning up behind themselves and other domestic tasks. Jewel also excelled in school from the beginning. In elementary school we were blessed to send Jade and Jewel to the Center for Creative Learning, a private school attached to a local church. This school was intense; the teachers were fully invested in the students and they prepared them to be able to handle a massive amount of challenging classwork and homework. This school offered small class sizes in a Christian learning environment. The school was for pre-kindergarten through the second grade. Jewel from day one tackled her work and was an assistant for her teachers and a helper to the other students.

Jewel was also a daddy's girl. Our children are so smart but sometimes they are too smart for their own good and we must steer them in the right direction. I can remember when Jewel was in the first grade and she figured out if she went to the school nurse and said that she was not feeling well then she could leave school early and her daddy would pick her up. Well, for three straight days I picked her up and had to continue my day, with her going to work with me and my coworkers loving that she was there, treating her extra special. We were getting lunch each day and then she was going home and just going along with her day like business as usual. I had to have a conversation with her and let her know the importance of her being in school and if she wasn't sick then she couldn't leave early. I explained to her the importance of taking her education seriously and even though I was having a good time spending time with her, she had to finish her full school day. She understood and I believe that having teachers and staff that cared was a major part of why she has done so well throughout the years.

Jewel attended a summer program at Bowie State University for cyber security in the summer of her junior year. It was a paid internship where she had to wake up and catch the Mark train at 7am and go to the program full-time, learn, and get paid. This was a program that she discovered on her own and committed to. She also entered Benedict College in 2019. She went to school early for their summer program to get an early start and to get acclimated with the school and environment. I think that was a mature decision since she was going to be five hundred miles away.

Jewel is an excellent example for her younger sisters. I'm immensely proud to be her dad. I love her energy and work ethic and look forward to supporting her success. No wonder she is in early childhood development; she has been directing her sisters since she was able to talk.

Jordan

Jordan is 13 years old and a great student, currently in seventh grade. She is an A student and participates in a lot of after-school activities. She is a part of the dance team and cheerleading squad, and she is also in an educational program called Higher Achievement, which she will remain in through high school.

Jordan Micah Jones was my baby girl for a long time, given the six-year age difference between Jordan and her older sisters. Starting off as a teenage parent to twin girls, Jade and Jewel were a new experience for me. I received on-the-job training with them. Now, with six years' experience and working a double the whole time, I was an expert, ready and excited for Jordan's arrival. Jordan's name was derived from my favorite basketball player Michael Jordan. The number one reason is because Michael Jordan's name is synonymous with greatness. I feel that three of my biological children look like me, but Jordan is my spitting image, just a more beautiful version. She had big, bright eyes, beautiful brown skin and was just a very pleasant baby. Jordan has always been full of life and personality. The great thing about Jordan was she had twin sisters who loved her and were already setting an excellent example for her. Jewel was a little more excited about Jordan's arrival. Jade was a little apprehensive because she was used to getting a lot of attention because they were twins and the babies of the family. Jordan has always made a strong impact in school. Her teachers just loved her and felt she was a great addition to their class. Jordan excels in her academics, but she always has been a part of dance troops, modeling camps, Girl Scouts, and gymnastics. She is an entertainer at heart, nonstop dancing. For a long time, Jordan would dance while she ate, dance when she woke, and create dance routines with her friends.

Every year for Jordan's birthday we alternate our celebration. One year we will have a party and celebrate with her family and friends. The following year she and I will pick a place for us to go and we take a mini vacation, just the two of us. Because she loves dance, one year we took her and the family to see what was at the time her favorite television dance group, Bring It, in Washington, DC for her birthday. She did not know up until the time when we were walking into the building. When the show was in progress, she was enjoying herself so much she was in tears. Wow, those are the moments that I live for.

Jordan, just like her name implies, will be great, and I'm enjoying every moment of her showing her greatness.

Brasela

Brasela is 10 years old, a great student, currently in fifth grade. She is an A student. Brasela is popular with her friends and is really focused on schoolwork. She loves to sing and entertain. She is highly creative; she loves to create art with her hands. We have plans to send her to an acting coach so she can end up on the big screen.

Brasela is my bonus daughter. When I found her mother and we became one, I was blessed to become her Padre, her bonus dad. One thing for sure, this girl is going to be a star. She has many talents, a big voice and an abundance of energy in a medium-sized package. I met Brasela when she was four years old and luckily, we had a good connection early on. I have been able to see her excel in school. She is consistently on the honor roll, even though the new grading system is a little different. The first half of the fifth grade she received straight A's in all her subject classes but because she had a few "Needs Improvement" on her report card she didn't make the principal's list. I'm still upset about that; obviously things have changed since I was in the fifth grade over 20 years ago. If you got straight A's, you accomplished the goal. So if you ask me, she is a straight A student.

Something that's very impressive about Brasela is that she is very business minded. She knows how to make money. I have seen her operate a candy business; she also had a slime factory in my basement, where she would make the slime at the house, take orders in school and distribute before and after school. It was going well until we found out that her business was doing so well that there were too many students putting in orders. It became a distraction, so we had to shut down the slime station and she has now moved on to her new passion, which is being a beautician. She took a summer course with girls that were 14 – 16 years old to learn how to become a hairstylist. It was a challenge for her because the older girls did not make her feel welcomed. But this was a time where we encouraged her, and she was mentally strong enough to push through and get the knowledge that she wanted out of the class. Now she hones her skills practicing on her mannequin and any and every family member who will let her style their hair. I have to say that the girl has skills.

I look forward to sharing in Brasela's success and supporting her along the way. Her Padre will always be there for her.

What is the Best Part of being a Father?

The best part about being a father is knowing that I have a direct impact on the future of this world—not from just my own efforts, but I'm also training and developing my children to be better than me: being there for them during challenging moments or times when they may be unsure if they can accomplish something; being their number one supporter to push them to be the best, but also letting them know that I'm going to love them either way, so they don't have a fear of failing. My daughters benefit from my experiences and the lessons that I have learned, the books that I have read and my perspective on the best way to navigate through life.

The fact that the same God who created everything saw fit for me to raise such powerful young ladies is mind-blowing. Watching your children grow in this life is like planting a garden. You start off with a small seed; you plant the seed in fertile ground and nurture the seed with water and the proper sunlight. That's the environment that you provide for your children: the knowledge, wisdom, and discipline. After a while you can see the seed grow into something beautiful that God intended. And that's what God intended for us as fathers, to be good managers of our children.

What a Child Needs Most from a Father

What a child needs most from a father is someone who is 100% invested in their child's future. A father should be willing to sacrifice in order to ensure his child's success in life. Whether it's supporting or disciplining, the action of love is especially important. So even when that teenager is not measuring up to your expectations, when they push you to your ultimate limit, love allows you to understand that life is not easy, we all make mistakes and the end goal is more important than the moment. I have been blessed with daughters who have been awesome over the years. But showing up when they are recognized for doing a great job in school or one of their extra-curricular activities, being there to support them and letting them know as their father, they make me proud—that goes a long way with a child and their confidence.

What I want to say to Black Moms

I want to shout out to black women and tell all the black moms out there, y'all ladies are really doing your thing in this new millennium. You're strong, you're creative, and fighting through many of the stigmas and stereotypes that you have endured while on your journey to gain your leading position in the professional world.

Even though there are hundreds of billions of venture capital funds distributed to new startup companies each year, there is literally a handful of black women who have received any of those funds. The exact number might as well be 0. The exact number from 2012 to 2014 is 24 out of 10,238 people who received this funding, which is 0.2 to black women. Still, with this disparity, black women in 2018 and 2019 opened 90 percent of the new women-owned businesses. These businesses experienced the highest rate of growth of any group during this period. Black women are also leading the charge in obtaining a college degree.

I would like to say we all salute your success but even though you are queens in your own right, we can go much farther together. A strategy of war is to divide and conquer. There has been a system set to break down the black family and it's hurting our children and increasing the economic wealth gap. You should take more time and make sure that the person you intend to have children with is the person who's demonstrating that he is the same man who wants to be with you and build a solid foundation with you, someone who is submitting to something that is higher than himself, so that he's not only loyal to you but he's held accountable to a higher power.

What is the most difficult part of being a father?

I would say co-parenting when the parents are no longer in a relationship with each other and they don't have the same vision for the child, the same end goal. It's a real challenge when there is division between the two parents; that only causes confusion for the child.

The two adults must put their differences aside and make sure that they are doing what's in the best interest for the child. Otherwise your children are caught in the middle and will find ways to leverage the fact that both parents are not on the same page; they will go back and forth between both parents, manipulating both sides for their own benefit. Children are super smart. They are always watching and taking mental notes. Self-preservation is a natural human trait so we instinctively, as we learn the environment and the system that we live in, learn how to survive and put ourselves in the best position for our own comfort. That's exactly what a child does in this situation; they will study the division and lack of communication by both parents and exploit them with a wide range of tactics that can often go unnoticed if you're divided. If you have multiple children, they can quite possibly work together to exploit the flaws in your coparenting strategy. To solve this dilemma your child's success should be worth you sacrificing your own feelings in order to work with the other parent and ensure your child/children can receive the guidance and discipline needed to guide them through life.

After six years with my biological children under the same roof, their mother and I separated and lived in different houses. Though starting our parenting off as teenagers, we figured out how to effectively raise our daughters and were blessed to have a supportive family to assist us through the challenges. But we put ourselves in a much more difficult position than if we had waited some time to learn ourselves, experience more life, and take a little more time to establish ourselves. By having children at such an early age, we were able to experience the joys of parenthood, but it also forced us into a lot of responsibilities and canceled our opportunity to live as free young adults.

What I gained from my Fathers

I know many people don't have a father in the household or even a father outside the house who wants to take responsibility and help raise their children. I was blessed to have a biological father who, even though he did not live in my household, was a major presence in my life. I grew up in Baltimore, MD, and my father Thomas Bacon and his side of the family lived in Philadelphia, PA. I would spend my summers in Philly and spend time with my dad, learning and studying how he operated as a man. I would go to work with him; he was a professional plumber and flipped houses. I didn't have an interest at the time in his work. I can remember going into dilapidated homes that he would acquire and turn into modernized new homes with amenities that you would see today on HGTV. Now the end-product, the fancy house, was cool at the time, but at the age of nine demoing a kitchen and replacing a floor was the exact opposite of what I wanted to do. Funny thing is, now, at the age of 38, I have a mortgage company and I'm a real estate investor. Go figure. I believe that him making sure that he picked me up and made me a part of his family, teaching me about life and how he maneuvered through it, directly impacted me in my parenting and outlook on life.

I was also blessed to have a stepfather in my life from the age of four, so I also had an example of a father in the home. I had the opportunity to look to him as a father figure as well. He was a dedicated deacon in our family church for the majority of my childhood. I was able to see him be faithful in his marriage to my mother for over 20 years. I also saw how consistency in working hard and being a good manager of your funds could benefit your life and take care of your family for the long term. We did not always see eye to eye, but later in my life I understood the challenge of being a bonus parent, taking on the child of someone that you love, as your own. In actuality, even though my mother and he had my younger brother when I was six years old, I was his first son. That is a big responsibility and a lot of that I didn't realize until I found my wife and became the bonus dad to Brasela.

I thank them both for helping prepare me to be the father that I am today.

Three things that I want black daughters to know

- If you have a father in your life or who is attempting to be in your life, who desires a relationship with you, even though your mom and your dad may not get along all the time, if he's reaching out then at least hear him out and use your best judgment. Fathers are important in your life; they can provide completion, protection and a standard that may be set. No one is perfect; we all need a chance, and maybe a second.
- Love God and follow the ways that the Bible has laid out for the process of selecting a husband, the roles of a wife and the position that your husband should have in the home.
- Everything you need you already have. Seek God's face; and be intentional in what you want and even clearer on what you don't want. So when either one presents itself, you know exactly how to handle the situation.

The legacy that I would like to leave behind for my children

- My children seeing me, over the years, live my life in a way that is pleasing to God.
- Always striving for success, being loving, caring and supportive of my families' dreams and aspirations. Another major part of my legacy is for my marriage to be a positive example for the youth.
- I would like to leave my children with knowledge of their family history.

- Household traditions that they can pass on to their families.
- I want to leave them with great memories of vacations with the entire family.
- I'm going to leave them with investments, multiple streams of income, a trust fund and a foundation that will operate globally, giving back to those in need, that they can manage. This will allow the generations to follow to start in a better position. As they go through life I would like to pass on the knowledge and wisdom that I've learned in and out of business.

Finally, what's important to me as a father

I feel that the black father's perspective is valuable. There are many fathers that are front and center, working every day to be the best example for the next generation, starting with their own children. Being a father can sometimes be a thankless job. My children's success is important to me as is each one of them feeling that I love them and will do what's needed to support them.

*"When you teach your son,
you teach your son's son."*

The Talmud

Wayne A. Mundell II is the founder of Nextlevel Training and Wellness. He has been a Certified Personal Trainer since 2002, after receiving his certification from the National Federation of Professional Trainers (NFPT). He is certified as a TRX Trainer, Athletic Performance Trainer, Nutrition Coach, and is also a Seated Massage Practitioner. Prior to his study of kinesiology at the University of Baltimore County, Wayne attended Catonsville Community College where he studied the dynamics of human behavior.

He integrates his knowledge and experience as a trainer and fitness specialist to design individualized, progressive training programs based on client health, strength, and fitness goals. He has an extensive background from training professional and amateur athletes, to training with everyday working professionals. Wayne has dedicated his time to coaching high school basketball and football, while also creating fun fitness with elementary school students in the surrounding community.

He has an innate ability to establish long-term and meaningful relationships with clients by helping them to integrate exercise and optimal wellness into the demands of daily life. His mission is to impact, inspire and create a community that lives a healthy and active lifestyle. Being centered in spirituality and a positive mindset is what fuels his commitment to leadership and passion to motivate those around him.

Wayne was born and raised in Baltimore, Maryland. He served as a firefighter and paramedic with the Baltimore City Fire Department for nine years. When he is not training or serving the community, he loves spending time with his daughters and family. He enjoys gardening, home improvement, and studying the aspects of personal development. Wayne's keen interest in entrepreneurship and professional advancement has given him the opportunity to collaborate with several businesses and non-profit organizations. He is dedicated to improving the world and serving others in a way that promotes holistic growth. He strongly believes if you can visualize success, then you can make it happen.

"Of all the titles I've been privileged to have, Dad' has always been the best."

Ken Norton

The Continuous Process of Becoming a Father

Wayne A. Mundell II

• • • • • • • • • • • •

I believe that being a father is a progression of worthy ideals. Any man can make a baby, but it is a continuous process to be a father.

The Genesis

My mother was a beautiful chocolate queen, short in stature, God-fearing, with a fiery spirit and a passion for helping others. She is a product of Jessup, Maryland, one of four siblings. She met my father when she was in high school, though they attended different schools. My father was a well-dressed, hardworking and ambitious young man from Elkridge, MD. He was one of six siblings and two foster children. Five years after my father escorted my mother to her prom, on a beautiful morning at Sinai Hospital on Aug 23, 1977, I was born.

When I was growing up, my parents' relationship was short-lived. I remember us living in a small apartment in Lansdowne, Maryland until I was four. Even though I was young, I have vivid memories of that time. I remember my neighbor; it seemed like he wore a white V-neck every day. Every time I saw him, he would speak like Donald Duck. I remember our living room: We had white furniture that we couldn't lie on for too long because back then all furniture was covered in plastic. I remember late night walks with my mother and father. I remember being on my father's shoulders as we walked the track at the high school, which was directly across the street from our apartment. I remember family time with my younger sister. I have tons of memories of those times.

Those memories would later influence my thought process as a father.

After my mother and father broke up, there was a common bond. I was a child with medical issues. I had childhood epilepsy and I would have seizures in school periodically. My parents had to come together when the time arrived for me to seek medical attention. I vividly remember them having to hold me down as the nurses administered IV treatment. "Let me see, let me see," I yelled, when the nurses were administering the IV; that is probably why I still have a fear of needles.

Even though my father did not live in the home with us, he had a huge influence on my thought process. Between the ages of eight and 14 years, we lived in East Baltimore. Our block was heavily influenced by the use and sale of drugs. The only reason why I was not consumed by the environment was because of my father. My father was super ambitious. He taught me the concept of never being ashamed of earning an honest dollar. My father showed me big money rolls and bank clips of money that he earned the legal way. That instilled in me the vision of entrepreneurship. He would get me on the weekends, and we would drive the neighborhoods. He would say, "Andre, take a look at that—do you see all that money?" I would look and see high grass or broken limbs or trash. But where most people saw a problem, he saw a solution. He saw that there was an opportunity to earn money landscaping or hauling things. He showed me at an early age that the world was a sea of opportunity; you just needed to be ambitious enough to go out and get it.

What are the best parts of being a father?

There are so many things that I've learned about myself as a man and who I want to be in this world, not only as a father but a contributor to mankind.

I became a father in 2010. Most of my friends and family thought that I would never have children. They had all had their children in their 20s. I was 32 years old when my daughter was born. Before that, I never really thought about having children or having a family.

I didn't think fatherhood was for me. However, now that I am a father, I can't imagine my life without my daughters.

When my daughter Kaleigh was born, I was 32, unmarried and in an off-and-on relationship. I was a firefighter and paramedic. I owned my own home and I had two businesses. It's interesting who you meet on your journey. My daughter's mother wasn't like anyone I had ever dated before.

The relationship ended soon after my daughter Kaleigh turned one. Then one year later, I was married, with a new baby girl, Lola.

My daughters are a blessing; they are a reflection of me. One of my daughters, Lola, is the free-spirited, compassionate, self-love version of me. Kaleigh is the coach, the leader, and takes charge. She is the aggressive side of me. The best part of being a father is listening to them and learning from them. I believe that we come into this world with a complete puzzle. We learn fear, we learn doubt, we learn uncertainty and those things scatter our puzzle pieces. I listen to them and see them not as just small children; they are little people who have their own ideas, visions, dreams, and aspirations. They allow me to connect with my inner child; they help me to be a free thinker. They allow me to be an explorer. I have learned that I am not here to just tell them what to do. I am here to be a guide and co-create with them.

Another amazing thing about being a father is that I get to love someone unconditionally. I have learned to be a better listener. I've learned how to manage anger and frustration. I've learned to be a better communicator. I have learned to trust God more from them.

What are the most difficult parts of being a father?

Co-parenting can be one of the most challenging parts of being a father. Getting the courts involved, not having the ability to agree to disagree, was one of the most difficult things I have had to experience as a father.

Not being able to see my daughters every day is an extreme challenge and is difficult for me. I have two daughters with two different women. My oldest daughter was with my ex-girlfriend and my youngest daughter is with my ex-wife.

In a perfect world, we would all put our differences aside and do what's best for the children. However, even saying that, what one thinks is best and what the other thinks is best may be two different things. So the difficulty is just learning to agree to disagree, having an open dialogue and/or creating buffers so things don't escalate.

When my parents broke up, I remember having to go to custody court and speaking with social workers. Having to choose who I wanted to live with was extremely hard for me. I remember both sides of the family saying negative things about each other.

I filed for custody of my oldest daughter, who is 10 now, when she was one or two years old. I filed several times with the courts; however, I could never go through with it because of the impact that it had on me when my parents went through a custody battle. I did not want my daughter to feel like I felt.

Black fathers usually have their hands tied when it comes to the court system. I never wanted to portray my daughter's mother in a negative light. I believe the courts make the environment a competition. To me, if that becomes the source and is built on power or control, no matter who wins, they both still lose.

How do you feel about single moms raising boys?

I think this is an extremely controversial question. A single mom can raise a child; however, she cannot raise a man. I know most of the female readers may find that a little offensive. But hear me out. I study psychology, and children don't do what you say: They do what you do. A woman can be an extraordinary parent, but she can never replace the identity of a man. Men and women bring special talents, special gifts that are God-given and unique. I believe a single woman raising boys should surround her boys with great male influence so they can see what a man is. My mother was a single parent, not a single mom. I lived with her; however, my father was in my life and showed me examples of what a man is.

As extraordinary as black women are, with their strength, power and grace, they are amazing examples of what a great mom is. Men and women have unique God-given skills and talents. We both have abilities that come naturally. I love the idea of equality in business, equality in opportunity, equality in finances, and equality in the world. However, men and women weren't designed to be equal in nature. We were designed to create balance within one another. Both women and men contribute something different that the other one does not possess.

You are born a male; however, you must become a man.

Understand this: There are four types of knowledge—learned knowledge, activity knowledge, modeling knowledge, and teaching knowledge. So a single mother can teach a boy what she thinks a man is; however, he must learn it, then do the activity, and the key component is modeling. He needs to model a man. Modeling is a divine principle. Every great teacher modeled a great teacher. This is no different.

What do you want the black daughter to know?

That they are beautiful. They are amazing. They are far greater than what the world may tell them they are. I am the father of two beautiful black girls. I instill the value of them knowing who they are. Not just by telling them—I make it a habit. I have instilled a simple daily morning routine: brush your teeth, wash your face, do your affirmations. Every day, I have them look at themselves in the mirror, look into the depths of their own beautiful brown eyes. They look and say, "I am beautiful. I am amazing. I am strong. God loves me. I love my ancestors. I am a millionaire."

I want all black daughters to believe in God's word. I want them to guard their hearts and minds and believe that God is with them, helping them and guiding them. I want them to believe the word that says that all things are possible to those that believe, that their God power is in how they use the Word.

I want black daughters to have unwavering belief in themselves, to see God inside themselves, to see the kingdom inside themselves. I want them to know that they are powerful, amazing and divinely created. When they have that type of belief in themselves, they will be able to conquer anything that life sends.

I want them to know that they don't need to fight to become equal with boys. That they are superior beings. When you are superior there is no need to compete. I want black daughters to have a divine understanding of who they really are. Learn how to self-soothe. Learn how to manage themselves with their emotions and manifest like magic.

What's your take on boys showing emotion?

I grew up with the mentality that boys shouldn't show any emotion. That they should just "suck it up and take it like a man." However, I grew up very angry, because I never fully learned how to express my emotions. I used to make and carry weapons. I would punch holes in walls, and kick furniture. I got into fights all the time because I never learned how to positively process my emotions.

I believe that the youth of today are hyper-emotional because they are told not to show emotion. You see, what is suppressed now becomes depressed. Depression creates disease. Disease creates disintegration. So when you see black boys angry, that is an emotion. However, the emotion of anger is a cover for the emotion of hurt. Hurt boys become angry boys. Angry boys become angry men. Angry men show their anger to cover up consciously or unconsciously the suppression of being hurt emotionally. I think young boys need to learn how to process their emotions. No emotion should be oppressed or suppressed. It should be expressed and processed.

If you look at some men today, whether they agree or disagree, they behave the same way that they did at an early age. They never learned how to process their emotions. Walking away, breaking things, throwing things are ways that some young boys learn to express their emotions. That same behavior will continue unless checked. So I think it's extremely important that young boys learn to show their emotions and learn how to properly process them, so it does not become suppressed.

Do you think that not having a father in the house affects a child negatively?

Well, that's a great question. I feel like if a man is toxic to the relationship of the mother and the child it will benefit the child if the father isn't in the home. One thing that I've learned in fatherhood and parenting is that kids don't do what you say, they do what you do. If the father is a negative influence in the home, more than likely it will negatively impact the child.

If the father isn't in the home or not present, I definitely believe it can have a negative influence on the mindset of a child. They can grow up feeling like something is missing or they missed out on something. Children need strong male guidance. A man's true nature is one of logic, reason and stability.

Those are the things that children need and are unconsciously looking for.

How important is co-parenting?

Just because the relationship ends doesn't mean that it's "The End." It's the beginning of a new one. The problems from the relationship don't just disappear. Tempers should go down and communication needs to go up.

Co-parenting can be extremely challenging, especially if there are wounds from the relationship that have not been resolved. This will impact how each parent handles themselves.

Great co-parenting is key. However, I never really saw a co-parenting relationship that I wanted to model in real life. It's troubling that our kids rarely get to see a man and a woman have a stable relationship. I believe that the ability to co-parent expands the scope of family.

The word "family" comes from the Latin word *famulus,* which means servant. I believe that everyone should be learning how to serve the unit as whole so that we all become better.

I took on bettering myself to become a better co-partner. I've learned a better way to communicate. I learned conflicts arise when there is a breakdown in understanding.

God gave me two ears and one mouth. I need to practice active listening and sometimes, saying less is more.

Simply asking yourself, "What could I do differently the next time?" will dramatically change the outcome. Now, this doesn't mean you're at fault or you did something wrong. However, I believe in 100/0. Taking 100% accountability and making zero excuses. You see, if I explore how I can respond differently then I will never be a victim to the same circumstance because I've changed. For things to change, you must change. For things to get better, you have to get better.

At the end of the day, the only thing you can control is the power of your own mind. The keen skill of responding instead of reacting and just simply setting aside your pride to give a sincere apology will go a long way.

I've been divorced for two years now, but I love the fact that my ex-wife actively maintains a relationship with my oldest daughter.

We make sure that the "sisters" don't miss a beat. We've had the ability to share co-parenting skills and she had me on her talk show. I believe that we are still a work in progress because we are constantly working on ourselves.

What type of legacy do you want to leave for your children?

I have several. However, the most important to me is the legacy of free thinking and self-confidence. I believe that anything can be achieved if you really use the power of your mind and have the confidence to apply it. I want to leave a legacy of health conscious-ness. You change how you think based on the level that you eat, the way that you take care of your body, the way that you take care of your spirit. Seeing yourself as a three-part being: mind, body and spirit. That's a legacy that I want to pass on to my children's chil-dren so that they have an awareness of who they truly are. I believe that true health starts in the mind.

Another legacy is to be wealth conscious. Wealth starts in the mind as well. Just like my father taught me, I want to teach my daughters that there is opportunity everywhere. We are surrounded by opportunity, but we need to be conscious enough to see it. The wealthy are our problem solvers. Teach them to use their God-given gifts and follow their purpose for life.

What do you want the world to know about black fathers?

That we do exist. There's an untrue narrative that's perpetually spread like a virus. I read that if you tell a lie or myth long enough that it will soon become accepted as the truth. There is a narrative in the world that says that there aren't many present black fathers, that black fathers aren't active in their children's lives, and that black fathers don't spend time with their children. That may be true for some, but that's not true for most. Most black fathers humbly do the task of being good fathers without recognition or celebration.

Black fathers are coaches, teachers, mentors, pastors, providers, doctors, lawyers, and leaders.

To all the black fathers, I salute you! Keep being great!

"Every father should remember one day his son will follow his example, not his advice."

Charles Kettering

 **Brian Horshaw** is a father, recording artist, worship leader, visual and performing arts instructor, actor, musician, songwriter, playwright, author, and motivational speaker. He has received various professional trainings from Catonsville Community College, Anne Arundel Community College, and Morgan State University. Brian has had many opportunities; including singing at prestigious events; acting in, directing and producing local plays; speaking at conferences; teaching in local public and private schools; and singing at churches throughout the nation. He received the Three Arts Club of Homeland Music Award in 2013, and performed at his very first live recording, "Light Up the Night" in 2014. His most recent achievements include the release of his first single, Anchored Hope, in 2017; and the development of the Xpressions Performing Arts Network. Brian is humbled to serve in such a capacity at such a young age and looks forward to the many opportunities that God has in store for his future.

Dear Seventeen-Year-Old Daughter

Brian Horshaw

• • • • • • • • • • • • •

To my beautiful daughter London, and to any other girl or boy who would like to read my thoughts.

I've spent useless time scrolling through my newsfeed on social media, viewing things like the greatest debate in all human history: "white dress with gold stripes?" or "blue dress with black stripes?" Reading the daily rants of first world-problems people were experiencing; inspirational quotes from my spiritual counterparts; and videos of bacon-stuffed, one-pound burgers that were deep fried and topped with cheese sauce.

But one day a post caught my eye that said, "What would you say to your seventeen-year-old self?" I thought long and hard about what I'd say to myself because I had quite a list. But the reality is, I can't talk to my seventeen-year-old self. As much as I'd like another chance to do some things over, the reality is I'm thirty-four and I can't undo the things that I'd like to redo.

But if I had a chance to speak to someone who is actually seventeen, or thirteen or twenty, maybe I could inspire someone with the limited knowledge I've acquired. Maybe I can give them a little bit of the wisdom that flows from the deep wells of my thirty-four-year-old self. The older I become, the more I learn and realize how not wise I am, and how much I do not know. I was asked in a recent interview if I would consider myself to be a leader. My response: "I don't know if I'd consider myself to be a leader in the context that other people view leadership. But if I am doing something that people see worth following, I welcome them to follow me on my journey."

My position in this writing is not that of author, but of student. I am learning life just like you are, and there's a lot that I do not know. Read with caution. I could share some things this go 'round that I may view differently in ten years. There may be some things in this book that you do not agree with, and that's okay. What works for me may not work for you. You must find your own path. In the words of my friend Denise, "Eat the meat and spit out the bones."

You are Loved

You are loved. This is something that I am trying to explain that I have not fully grasped yet, but if you can own this at a young age, it will set an amazing foundation for your life.

"We accept the love we think we deserve." – Stephen Chbosky

Whoo! Halleluyer, thank ya Stephen! Someone take up an offering for this man because he's so correct.

I am grateful for and will pay homage to my religious upbringing in another chapter, but can I first start off by saying religion effed me up? Pardon my French. It was the blessing that was also the curse because I always felt like there was something wrong with me—that I was always doing wrong. That I would have to do the right things to correct my wrong things. But when I would try to do the right thing, I'd end up doing the wrong thing, thus producing two wrong things instead of just one wrong thing. One can only imagine how exhausting that can be. I did not feel right unless I felt wrong. There was just this heavy seed of guilt and shame that grew and spread like weeds in my life over time. I am still working on this, might I add.

And here is the thing folks: I grew up Methodist, so it's not like I was a part of an extremely rigid religion. I didn't have to confess my sins to a priest or anything, or crawl on my knees until they bled to pay for my sins...yes, this is a real thing that people still do today. Please look it up; it is staggering! I went to what I would consider a normal Methodist church with other normal people. But for some reason, I had a strong focus on the sin in my life, while I should have just been enjoying being a kid.

This weed spread to other areas of my life. I only felt loved by God if I was doing the "right" things. I only felt loved and accepted by peers if I did what they wanted me to. I wanted acceptance from family, friends and colleagues, so I pretended to be who they wanted me to be. I had to work hard for love. I had to fight for love. I had to pretend for love. My identity had to change from group to group for acceptance. My life's mission was to receive love. And when you want something bad enough, you will do anything to get it—even if it's the wrong thing—because you just want to be loved.

I have done things that crush me to talk about. Like having sex outside in the cold snow, and meeting someone new to have an intimate encounter with just about every day of the week, just to feel something that felt like love and acceptance.

But the problem was, I did not know that I was already loved. I was told that I was loved by God, but I did not know it. I had a head knowledge of His love from what I was told, but I didn't have a heart knowledge of it. I didn't know that I was loved more than ever by God. I did not know that I didn't have to earn it. I did not know that it could never be taken away. I didn't know that I didn't have to fight or pretend to get it. I did not know that I could be a complete mess and seen as the most valued person on Earth.

Not having an understanding of the treasure of God's love is like someone leaving you an inheritance of twenty-million dollars and it is sitting in another account. But you don't know that account is there, so you live day-to-day in poverty, struggling, paycheck to paycheck.

I accepted the love I thought I deserved. I thought I deserved to be loved by God based on my actions. I thought I deserved love from others if I met their expectations. And this view of love translated to the type of love I gave myself. I didn't love myself. Because how can I love me, if God doesn't love me? And how can I love me if others don't love me?

Dear seventeen-year-old daughter, or whoever is reading this book, this is why I put this as the first portion of my chapter, because this is the foundation of how we live our lives and the way we see the world, and the choices that we make. Before we teach our kids how to read and write, or anything else, we must teach them that they are loved. Imagine how many suicide bombings we would avoid if that person who committed the act knew they were loved, and they didn't have to earn it by taking the lives of others. If you can get and grasp that, you will be unstoppable!

I love and look up to Willow and Jaden Smith. People have criticized them for being weird, strange, rebellious—you name it. But they don't care. That's what I love about them…they just don't care! Their security is completely independent of others. My, how I wish I were able to take on such a disposition when I was their age. As teenagers, they know they are loved, and they love themselves even if no one else does; and the result of that love is freedom! Freedom to be you! There is nothing more exhausting than trying to be someone other than yourself. God made you like you on purpose! If God wanted you to be someone else, He would have made you someone else. Your skin color, hair texture, voice, abilities and talents, strengths and even weaknesses were hand-crafted by the maker of the universe on purpose!

So you—yes, you! With all your flaws, weaknesses, insecurities, mistakes, bad choices, future bad choices… you're awesome. Forgive yourself. Let it go. Don't sweat the small stuff and make a decision to let go of even the big stuff. You are not responsible for living up to the expectations of others; and other people's opinion of you is none of your frickin' business!

You are loved. And if you don't have a heart knowledge of that love, make it your life's mission, on purpose, every day, for however long it takes, to accept and receive that love. Then you'll know what love is, and you won't accept anything less than that. Not from others, not from the God who gives love based on merit that you've fabricated in your head, not even from yourself. And I believe what the great Whitney Houston said with all conviction that "learning to love yourself is the greatest love of all," because that's where the freedom comes! Don't accept the love you think you deserve. Accept the love you actually deserve. Learn to love even the most unpleasant parts of yourself. You are loved. Now be free!

God

I mentioned before that I would touch on this subject. Please know that my perspective is one of someone who has been in church all his life yet is still learning who God is. My views that I place in this book could evolve in a few years as I experience and teach Him more.

God… The mysterious one. Invisible, yet all the signs add up that He is there. People all over the world and throughout time have searched and wanted to know exactly who this mysterious spirit is. You're not alone in this search. Throughout the Bible, you'll find stories of people who are genuinely inquisitive about God's identity. They are confused about who He is and what to call Him. You'll see that some people in the Bible based their beliefs on what they'd been taught in a particular region during a specific time. You'll find beliefs from one region mixed with the beliefs of another region, forming a new set of beliefs, and even people converting from one belief to another.

Today, we have estimated about forty-two-thousand religions in the world, most of which are subdivisions of a major religion. For example, in Christianity alone, there are Baptists, Catholics, Methodists,

Episcopalian, African Methodist Episcopalian (AME), Assemblies of God, Presbyterian, Lutheran, Pentecostal, Evangelical, Church of God In Christ, Seventh-Day Adventist, Jehovah's Witnesses... and these are just a few of the ones that I know of off the top of my head. All these Christian denominations use the Bible to justify what they believe to know as truth, yet their denominations separate them from other denominations because they are not in agreement as to what that truth is. Confusing, right?

Please forgive me if the next part of what you read is a little boring but trust me it's necessary for my point. The Bible is a collection or library of books written by men and believed to be divinely inspired by God. These books were written for the people living in specific regions during specific times, yet I believe the book is timeless in its application of the principles and wisdom, and even relevant in terms of its apocalyptic literature. Scripture was recited mostly orally in Biblical times because many people couldn't read or write, and the supplies to write large documents were quite expensive. Copies of manuscripts that were written were found over time, cross-referenced and tested for accuracy. These books were put together in a process known as canonization. There was a strict vetting process that was determined by a group of men at the Council of Carthage in AD 327 who determined which books we should have in our Bible. Catholic Bibles include other books that are not a part of the Protestant Bible, as those additional books were not accepted by Jews or Protestants. These books were then translated over time from language to language, and some words have been changed to other words that have completely different meanings. Translations have been influenced by politics, culture, psychology, religion, military, and there is still uncertainty as to what some of the original

Hebrew and Greek words actually mean. ALL THAT TO SAY that the search for truth can be confusing and ambiguous. Who is God? What is truth? How do we know if truth is truth if they say truth is truth; and we say truth is truth, both pulling from the same source of truth, yet we don't agree on what is true?

Here is my position. Be ready to eat the meat and spit out the bones. I believe that God wanted us to know a few things about Him and how to live our lives in a way that honors Him. I believe that He inspired people to write these things down so that they would serve as instruction and examples. God is not flawed, and neither are His words. But humans are flawed creatures. Therefore, I feel like some (not all) of the writings of the Bible do present a bias from the author and culture of that time. I believe that translations have error due to misunderstanding of text and have a bias from the translators, other influences, and the culture of the time in which it is being translated. In conclusion, our modern-day Bible is subject to error, but I do believe it's the closest thing we have to God's original message.

But even with the Bible, I feel like it compartmentalizes God and His character. How can one book or a collection of sixty-six books really tell us about the fullness of who He is? I mean the biography of Jesus' thirty-three-year life was summed up in a few books.

Dear seventeen-year-old daughter or whoever reads this book, I encourage you to use the Bible as a foundation, but I also encourage you to get to know Him for yourself outside of the book. Every day I seek to know this mysterious spirit, and some things that I thought I knew about Him from religion or society, I'm finding are not who He is at all. Religion in its good intention is such a flawed system. In my search for who God is, I'm learning to take him out of the religious box that says, "you must do this" or "you mustn't do that" to know, have a relationship with, or be accepted by God. I'm learning that God is love. He wants to love us. He wants us to love Him back. He wants us to spread that love to others.

One of the teachers of religious law was standing there listening to the debate. He realized that Jesus had answered well, so he asked, 'Of all the commandments, which is the most important?'

Jesus replied, 'The most important commandment is this: Listen, O Israel! The LORD our God is the one and only LORD. And you must love the LORD your God with all your heart, all your soul, all your mind, and all your strength.' The second is equally important: 'Love your neighbor as yourself.' No other commandment is greater than these. – Mark 12:28-31 (NLT)

There you have it folks, words from Jesus himself! And while this is only a small passage of scripture in the Bible, I feel like it's probably the most important. I think it highlights the essence of who God is and who we should be. He is love. We should give love. Love God. Love people. And it makes sense! I mean, how different would the world be if we loved God and truly loved others? Maybe we would all be in Heaven if that happened. Maybe that's what Heaven is like?

I've also found that no matter how complex God is or how complicated humanity has made it to connect with Him, I know that we need Him. We are spiritual creatures, and if you ever study humans in general you will see that there is a deep longing and essential need to connect with our creator.

I've found that this connection is vital, and I can always feel when I'm disconnected. I connect best through music, meditation and being in nature. There's something about being around a body of water where I can just feel God's presence. Connecting with my creator raises my frequencies and something about feeling His love makes you feel beyond amazing! In whatever way you feel you connect best, make it your effort every day to get to know God. Don't complicate it. Don't put Him in a box. Get a heart knowledge of who He is, and heart knowledge of His love. God is love. You are loved.

Be Ghetto

"Finding yourself" is not really how it works. You aren't a ten-dollar bill in last winter's coat pocket. You are also not lost. Your true self is right there, buried under cultural conditioning, other people's opinions, and inaccurate conclusions you drew as a kid that became your beliefs about who you are. "Finding yourself" is actually returning to yourself. An unlearning, an excavation, a remembering who you were before the world got its hands on you. – Emily McDowell

I think parents have a plan of who and how their kids will be before they are even born. For example, I had already made up in my mind once we found out that your mom was pregnant that you would be a boy. "No penis in there," said the lady giving us the sonogram. Turns out you weren't a boy, but in fact a girl, and the greatest girl that a dad could ever ask for. But isn't that how it is? Don't we come up with these ideal situations for just about everything and everybody?

Korean comedian and actor Ken Jeong spoke in his stand-up special about how he had to break it to his parents that he didn't want to be a doctor anymore, but instead a stand-up comedian. He didn't have any family support. His dad had plans for him to be a doctor before he was born. When he broke the news to him, his dad began cursing in Korean and telling him how he brought great shame to their family. He is one of many examples of how parents have decided the paths for their children without giving them the opportunity of finding their own. I've seen it in church. Dad's a pastor; granddad was a pastor; son, you shall also be a pastor. There are ideals in families, cultures, social circles and so on. I ashamedly admit, I had my own ideals for you. I just knew you'd be a poised, well-mannered, proper-speaking, high-achieving, disciplined little girl who would be the poster child of the kid that everyone wanted their kid to be like.

When you were only four months old, I noticed a little feistiness about you, and I noticed it even more as you got older. You weren't poised. You were wild, free, and had no worries in the world. You took risks and were fearless. You'd smack your food loudly, get food all over your mouth, scream in excitement, laugh obnoxiously loudly, and were just plain fun.

You were three years old attending a highly conservative Christian school and you got in trouble almost every day, to the point where you had to sit in the principal's office all day for really just being yourself. After that horrible private school experience, I put you in a high-performing school whose demographic consisted of 68% Caucasian students. Not only did you suffer from not appreciating your own identity because of the indirect whitewashing from your peers, but you probably suffered from me as well.

I had this big disgust for "ghetto girls." I couldn't stand the attitude; I was repulsed by the use of improper English. I was annoyed by the loudness, need for attention, and lack of what I considered to be good home training. But even though I put you in conditions that I felt would make you...not ghetto, I came to the revelation that my daughter was quite "ghetto."

"Don't be ghetto," "Don't talk ghetto," "Don't act ghetto like such and such," I'd tell you. Even some of the entertainment that was harmless, that you genuinely enjoyed, I didn't want you watching because I didn't want you to end up like those "ghetto girls."

And this is just one of many things I got wrong as a parent. When we'd go out, I'd have to freshly do your hair. "Don't spill food on your clothes," because I think I subconsciously had this idea of perfection for you. Oh, what a wretched soul I am. I was pushing my ideals on you, ineffectively socially conditioning you to be who I thought you should be. Please forgive me, seventeen-year-old daughter, for telling you who you should be or how you should be. Like Emily McDowell said, you already knew who you were. Who am I to take that away from you? Who am I to dilute your awesomeness and dull down your personality to the things that make you, you?

I remember now. My parents had their ideals for me, and all I wanted to do was be myself. It's amazing how we can take something negative that happened to us and pass it down to our children.

So, my seventeen-year-old daughter or anyone who reads this book, my message to you is to "BE GHETTO!" Be extroverted, be introverted, be good at art, be bad at art, be poised, be wild. Be whoever it is you are. My seventeen-year-old daughter, be who you were before I got my hands on you. You're only nine years old as I'm writing this. But as I type with tears flowing down my eyes, I am so, so proud of the person you are. You amaze me every day by merely existing. I would love to say that I can't wait to see what you'll become because I know it will be something great, but I can't say that, because you are already great! Your existence inspires, and influences so many people including me. God knew exactly what He was doing when He created you, with your amazingly ghetto-fabulous self! God is love. You are loved. So be who He made you to be, even if you have to piss people off in the process.

Two Rails

Life is like a set of parallel train tracks, with joy and sorrow running inseparably throughout our days. – Kay Warren

Imagine being a train…crazy analogy, I know, but just stick with me. Let's say that the train track you're on is "life." On the left side of the track there is happiness. And on the right side of the track is sorrow. You cannot derail the track, so your only choice is to experience both at the same time. Isn't that how it works?

I'll tell you how my two-sided track is looking right now. I'm writing this in the middle of the COVID-19 crisis…right rail. I'm currently unemployed…right rail. But neither I nor any of my family members have tested positive for the virus…left rail. And I have a job opportunity to deliver packages because that's the only industry that seems to be hiring right now... left rail. But this is nowhere on the map of my well-planned career path... right rail. But the time being stuck in the house has really allowed me to enjoy the simple things, and time with you and our family...left rail. Got an idea how it works?

Happiness. It's something that everyone longs for. Some people think that the guy will make them happy. Or the family will make them happy. Or the house will make them happy. Or the career will make them happy. Or to be included with that group will make them happy. Or that money will make them happy—only to find that none of those things make them happy. Or that it makes them happy, but only temporarily. This is why you see some celebrities turn to drugs, or commit suicide, because all the money and luxury in the world still leaves them with a void.

In the beginning of the book of Ecclesiastes, King Solomon talks about how he had everything. He had status. He was rich. He had slaves. He had many wives, houses, food, entertainment, wine... all the things that fire off happy chemicals in our brains. But he came to the conclusion that having every good earthly thing was all "meaningless" and that his pursuit of these things is like "chasing the wind."

I think happiness is abstract. I don't believe "happiness" exists by itself, because sorrow is always going to be there. I believe King Solomon had a two-railed train track of his own. Even though he had all he could ever want, I bet that there were some things in his life that fell on the right side of the track. He had the pleasures of life; but considering he was a melancholic alcoholic, I'm willing to bet he had his share of sorrow too.

So what do we do with this two-railed track that we cannot derail? I think that we should choose joy. But what does that mean? And isn't it a lot easier said than done?

I believe that happiness comes from our circumstances. It's an outward-in experience. "Oh look, cake!" Now I'm happy! Outward-in. But joy, on the other hand, is an inward-out sense of being.

Some friends of mine went on a mission trip to Kenya, and they mentioned how poor the conditions were in the villages that they were visiting. They had sheets as doors, and a mat lying on a dirt floor that four people slept on in a one-room house. In scorching hot temperatures, they had no air conditioner, and none of the modern conveniences that we have here in the US.

"I stood there confused and I felt so selfish," my friend Jeff explained, "because they were so nice, and happy, and they looked out for each other, and they praised God with joy, yet they had nothing. And here I am in my hotel with my air-conditioner, irritated because the Wi-Fi is not working."

How is it that the people of Kenya that my friend Jeff told me about could have nothing, but be so joyous? Because joy is an inward-out sense of being. A village stricken with poverty, famine, and disease, yet they praised God with joy despite what was "happening." Dear seventeen-year-old daughter or whoever reads this book, I believe that joy comes from God.

I am leaving you with a gift—peace of mind and heart. And the peace I give is a gift the world cannot give. So don't be troubled or afraid. – John 14:27 (NLT)

Remember in section one when I said that God's love is like having twenty million dollars in another account that we don't know that we have? I feel like that's the same with all God's gifts. We search, and fight, and medicate, and cope because we are in search of a gift that the world cannot give. We search for happiness when it is conditional upon our happenings. And if it's conditional upon our happenings, then that means that there is always going to be pain, sorrow, and grief running simultaneously on that right rail. In essence, happiness apart from sorrow doesn't truly exist.

You are going to have some really awesome experiences, but you are also going to go through some really hard things. Some things will be unimaginable, and you'll question if you'll be able to get through it. But if you can choose to be joyous like the people of Kenya and receive the amazing gift of joy and peace that is an inward-out state of being, you will find that you can have the joy and the peace of God, even when it seems as though the train is leaning heavily on the right side.

But how do I get this peace and this joy? The real answer to your question is "I don't know." I don't know if I have a magic formula for that. For me I think it starts with a determination to have joy. I believe it's something that I can have, and I actively pursue it. I purposely find things to be grateful for. I take the joy and the peace that I have, and I share it with others. There's something about doing something nice for other people who can't do a thing for you. It shows you and them that God is still doing good things. I find songs and I read things that remind me of who God is and His promises. I reflect on the past and how God came through for me, and that encourages me that He'll come through again.

Dear seventeen-year-old daughter or anyone who reads this book, life is so amazing in the sense that you will experience pain, grief, sorrow, lamentation, ugly, cold, bitter, and darkness. But you'll also experience laughter, smiles, pleasant smells, great food, fun experiences, love, and memories. And through it all you can have joy. God is love. You are loved. Be who He created you to be and experience His joy.

To be continued...

Little did I know that one day someone would want to read my thoughts, find them interesting, and want to publish them so that other people could read them also.

There's so much more I want to share. These are just a few of my thoughts that came first. Hopefully, you enjoyed a few pieces of meat and spit out very few bones. I just may continue with my thoughts in a full book that will contain a lot of what I didn't get a chance to say here.

Continue to grow and be a life-long-learner; and be willing to unlearn some of the things that you were sure of at one point. Till then, God is good. You are loved.

 **Kenneth Gilmer** is a father to four beautiful daughters and a grandfather of six. He was Born and raised in Maryland. Mr. Gilmer graduated from Old Mill Senior High School in Millersville, MD in 1983. He Served in the United States Airforce and the Army National Guard. Kenneth is currently a service manager in the pest control industry. He serves as an Elder in a local church in Eastern Shore Maryland. He currently resides in Glen Burnie, Maryland with his wife of 29 years.

DADDY'S GIRLS

KENNETH GILMER

. . . .

Let me introduce myself. I'm a 55-year-old African American (black) father of four girls, who've turned out to be four of the most beautiful, spirited women of today. Might I add, they mean the world to me. I remember back when I was growing up, I never thought I would ever be a father let alone to four girls. To be exact, I wasn't planning on becoming a father, I just wanted to have fun being me. You know, just being responsible for myself only. The whole idea of being a father really made me feel uneasy. Why? Because the thought of someone depending on me to care for their wellbeing was unimaginable. Who knew? I can say this, that being a black male raising children was both challenging and rewarding. Honestly, black males becoming fathers in this era is a task that must be met with compassion, understanding, and humbleness. Oh yeah, and throw in some flexibility.

There are some exceptionally well put together black fathers, and here's my spin on this. As I said I'm the proud father of four beautiful women. We all know that raising girls to become respectful women is no easy task. I had to be a nurturer, always encouraging them to follow their dreams. I had to be a protector, by guarding them physically, emotionally, and spiritually. When I say physically, it means picking them up when they fall; when I say emotionally, to be able to carefully speak to their hurting heart; and when I say spiritually, I should be able to speak words of strength to their soul.

In being a father, I realized that I had to be a leader in their life, not to dictate their life but to educate them on how to maneuver through each phase of their life. Now anybody knows, with daughters that's no easy ride. To tell you the truth, it was an everyday learning experience. I didn't want to be just a good father, I wanted to be an effective father. To me that would be the crown of fatherhood. As a father I want to deposit tangible substance to achieve promising results in their lives.

There's another part of me being a father, and that is raising a child that's biologically not mine. Let me say this to any man who's in this position: Love them deeply. Never have I made my oldest daughter feel like she's the other child. I would always reassure her of who she was to me, so I removed the word step from daughter; it just didn't fit. I let her know that as long as I have breath in my lungs, she will never hear me call her my stepdaughter.

When I achieved being an effective father; then and only then, could I stand on the phrase, *anyone can be a father, but it takes a special sort of man to be a daddy.* You see, I like being a daddy; it has taught me to lead by example. I wanted my influence in my daughters' lives to maximize every effort in them to achieve their goals in life. I challenged them to keep pushing and told them that nothing was out of their grasp. I would encourage them to meet each obstacle head-on, standing tall. I taught them that every failure that they endured would be just a minor pause in their life, but to regroup with a better perspective. I look at them today and marvel at the women they have become. Like I said, this whole daddy thing caused me to be an innovator, have a sense of humor about things that might have flipped the average dad out. I want to be a positive role model to my girls. I said before, being a dad has taught me how to effectively communicate with my girls, how to have patience, to walk with confidence so that they can also. I also learned a lot of compassion for them and how they move through this day and season. Being a dad, there was always room for development not only as a man but as a man being a dad. My vision always had to be clear, not just for me but for the entire family. Being a dad, I wanted to always shield them from things this world would throw at them. Boy oh boy, one of the most uncomfortable moments that would put any father in defense mode is the mention of liking boys. Now any dad will agree with me that that day felt like time just stopped for a moment. Maybe the reason is because we are men also and know the game that's going to be played. There were a lot of days of inhaling and exhaling. You might think I walked a tight rope— nope. Boy, did I make mistakes in this parenting thing. Getting things right was a challenge in itself. At times I would overreact about a situation and cause it to be bigger than it should've been. Man, the growing pains of fatherhood.

One of the biggest lessons that was taught not only to my girls but to me as well was to own up to it and make it right. There was never a dull moment around here. Being a father is a never-ending learn- ing experience. My only goal was to develop strong, independent black women. I would always tell them to get theirs, never totally rely on a man for anything, always stack their own so that any man who comes into their life, what they bring would complement what they already had. I would say to them, "Tell yourself that you are beautiful so if a man tries to use that, say thank you but I know that I am because my daddy tells me all the time." That's right, I tell my girls all the time that they are beautiful black queens on this earth and to never settle for less. Being a father has taught me that I have to live what I preach to them—like I said earlier, lead by example.

Looking at all of this, I have to give a shout out to my mom. Believe it or not, she is the one true reason I am the man I am today. Come to think of it, she is the one who gave me core values that constructed the very foundation I based my parenting skills on today. The endless, selfless sacrifice that I witnessed in the home she built with love, guidance, compassion, and wisdom was and still is priceless. It was the strength that was shown even in the worst times that gave me the will to emerge as the father I am today. THANK YOU, MOM!

Trust me, there were men who played key roles in my life, and kudos to them, but the top honors go to the diamond on earth and that's my mom. Watching how she raised me and my siblings gave me the blueprint to formulate a strategy in raising mine. She held it together by constantly progressing, instilling in me to always keep reaching. Now did my mom settle for anything less from me. No, not a chance. When the potential was raised, and she would see me slip, she would pull me up and let me have it straight. I have allowed that to saturate the very core of my parenting skills. This is for all single mothers out there: I say thank you in advance and keep raising the bar on the young sons in your home. You can do it (sorry fellas, I had to say that).

This brings me to my next. To put the special touch on me being a father/daddy is when I found God. This role was a tremendous revelation into who I really am as a man and as a father. I learned some things about myself that brought about a change in me. What I thought about fatherhood, God took me deeper into myself. I realize that I was built for this. For me it was a restructuring of the exterior of the blueprint of my version of fatherhood. I wanted to be more than just a good father; even more so, I wanted to go past being effective at it. To do this I realized I had to be more of a transformational father. What do I mean by that? In order to do what I said earlier I had to first look within myself and begin to encourage and motivate myself to truly embrace the challenge of fatherhood. I know it seems that I may sound like I'm off focus but believe me, I'm focused.

Let me explain what I mean by embracing fatherhood. Accepting being or becoming a father will keep you from going through the motions of being a father. I wanted to be more than just a presence. I wanted to be a father who encouraged the motivation and positive development of my girls, to exemplify moral standards and encourage the same in them. I just couldn't be that father who only gave just something. I wanted to be that father who gave all that I had and then reached deep down and gave again. Being a dad is a responsibility and role that every man who is, or wants to be, shouldn't take lightly.

I feel that now my vision is becoming clearer. If my vision is clear than I can instill that in my children. You see, when I found God, I realized He is the ultimate Father figure. In Genesis, God says to be fruitful and multiply—well, that's what I intend to do. Multiply what's on the inside of me and instill it into my girls. To find joy in everything, even in bad times. Continually imparting, planting, depositing what they need to navigate through life. Again, to lead by example. Currently this very moment in time isn't 'do as I say'; it has become 'do as I do.' Children start to emulate you—no, imitate the very things you do—so it's very imperative that we as fathers be that positive role model for our children, especially if we are raising girls. As fathers raising girls, we should be the first love of our girls. I knew the type of man I used to be, and I didn't like it at all when my girls came on the scene. Believe me when I say this: I gave their boyfriends the blues. Being a father, I would do it all over again. I wouldn't trade it for anything in the world. I have been rewarded repeatedly. To see them as they are now, I'm amazed at what is in front of me. I truly thank God for the ability to go through this and if any man out here thinks that being a father is a right then you are sadly mistaken. You better get this embedded in your senses: Being a father is a privilege and a great responsibility.

In the beginning I said that I had four daughters, but I only had the opportunity to raise just two of them. Now did it hurt to not be able to have a hand in raising my other two. You bet it did. It felt like a major piece of me was ripped away. I remember my mom would tell me, "We will see them again." Well she was right, 19 years later my other two daughters are back in my life and I love the steps that are being made to build a bridge to a meaningful relationship between a father and his daughters. I can say this: When you pray to God, be ready for what comes. I thank Him for the second opportunity to be in their lives. The amazing thing is, they didn't come back into my life at the same time but at the right time. My first middle daughter lived in another state and she wanted to attend a college right here closer to us. When she arrived at the airport accompanied by her mom and dad, I was nervous and emotional. I had to fight back the tears. You see, I hadn't seen her since she was a baby. To see her all grown up was bittersweet. Fast forward, we have a good stable relationship. Thank you, Jesus, for your promises to me. Wait, I'm not done. My other middle daughter reached out to me by way of her aunt, and the rest is history. I'm truly blessed to have them in my life. Okay, I know there's this question, I can feel it from you: What about the mothers? The question is, what about them? Trust me, I don't have not one bad bone in me for them. They did exactly what was needed and what I prayed for and that was that my daughters would grow into strong black women and that's what materialized in front of me. So for that, I'm grateful for the results. There isn't room to bash anybody. My goal is to be here for them as much as I am for the other two.

To sum it all up for me, I will be that transformational father who transforms into an exceptional dad, to lead and guide my children to be the best that they can ever be. I will cheer them on constantly and love them. I will continually build them up and keep pushing them to be great in every aspect of their lives.

 **Gary A. Johnson** is the President of Gary A. Johnson Company & Associates, a management training and consultant firm for the federal government and Fortune 500 companies. He's also the Founder & Publisher of Black Men In America.com, ranked as one of the top websites for African Americans, and the owner of MasterChef Gary's Premium Organic Seasoning. Gary is also the author of the book, "25 Things That Really Matter In Life: A Comprehensive Guide To Making Your Life Better." Gary quit his job to be a "Stay-At-Home" Dad when his two sons were 4 and 7 years old. Gary's been married to the same woman for 35 years.

Call Me Dad

Gary A. Johnson

* * * * * * * * * * * * *

There is a big difference in being a father and being a dad. Being a father is critically important; after all, that's the start of life. Being a dad is a lifelong rollercoaster ride that never ends. The emotional investment required to be a dad is exhausting, challenging and rewarding, sometimes all at the same time. The dads who are "in it to win" never quit on their children and they NEVER stop loving them. That's what makes the "job" so important.

My perspective on being a father started with my father, Samuel H. Johnson. His mother had him when she was a teenager and he grew up without a father in his life. One of his goals was to be the best father that he could be. He didn't have his father in his life, but he did have positive male role models in his life, and he ended up being a great role model for me. To give you some additional perspective, when I got married, my father was my Best Man. That should tell you everything you need to know about his influence in my life.

I grew up in a stable two-parent household with a younger sister in Washington, DC. Both of my parents worked their government jobs until retirement. We were not rich, but looking back, I got all my basic needs met. For years, our family car was a taxicab, one of my father's three jobs. I remember my father started giving me advice when I was around 10 years old, advice that I can recall and rely on today. Pearls of wisdom like:

- All you need in life is one good friend.
- Never start anything in a relationship that you're not willing to keep doing or maintain.
- When you get married, listen to your wife and do what you must do to maintain the relationship. Don't take the advice of your friends over the advice of your wife.
- Never embarrass your wife in public and keep certain things between the two of you and not in the street.
- Never put your hands on a woman in anger. If you get mad or upset, leave the house or go for a walk.

I have been married for 35 years to the same woman and I have been an active father to our two sons. In fact, I quit my successful government job to be a "stay-at-home" dad when my boys were four and seven years old.

I believe that spending quality time with my family will extend the quality of my life. Parenting is the most important, the most difficult job I will ever have in my life. You are never NOT a parent, even after your children grow into adulthood and leave the house.

The responsibility of molding and shaping another human being's life is one of the most important tasks that you can have. Developing a strong emotional connection with my sons was paramount.

Providing a safe environment and happy existence and making each son feel special and loved was difficult. Growing up, I treated my sons differently, because they are different. However, despite the different treatment, I strived to treat them fairly and equitably.

I would like to share my perspectives on being a Dad in the following modular or "bite-sized" chunks: Communication, Role Modeling, Health & Wellness, Legacy, Final Thoughts and some worksheets.

Communication

An effective communicator must be able to show emotions, be vulnerable and apologize to your children when you are wrong or make a mistake. I made mistakes as a dad. Children are little people with feelings. Words and deeds matter. When you are wrong or hurt their feelings, sometimes you must apologize. One of the goals of parenting is not showing your children that you are better than they are but doing those things that will develop them to be caring, empathetic and a productive member of society.

You want to talk to your children in a way that is "hearable." The best way to accomplish this is to spend time with them and get to know the strengths and areas that are challenging for them that can be improved. You should only give your children feedback to help them get better and not to tear them down.

Kids have dreams. You should not impose your limitations or goals on your children by killing or squashing their dreams. It is a delicate balance, but instead of squashing their dreams, you can introduce some reality and perhaps help your son or daughter develop a strategy to accomplish their goals. One of the worst things you can do is to tell children that they can't do or become something. Why place shackles on them? Always seek to help them excel.

Role Modeling

I was born to be a dad. As early as high school, I can remember thinking that one day I would be a dad and I always believed that I would be a good dad. Having a good relationship with my sons and now my granddaughters is one of the most important factors for my happiness and stability. The best gift that a man can give to his children, in addition to spending time with them, is to model the appropriate behavior consistently.

One way to model behavior and cultivate and sustain a solid relationship with your children is to spend quality time with them. Turn off the television, leave work early, and invest your time where you will get the most return, which is with them.

From the time my sons were infants, I took them everywhere I went. I set up a workstation at my office and home office for them. We worked, laughed, talked and played every day. One of my fondest memories is watching my children laugh. When children are laughing, all is right with the world.

Modeling the appropriate behavior is another way of teaching our children values. My children had a front row seat to how I treated their mother (my wife), my mother, my sister and how I treated myself in terms of my own health and wellness.

Health & Wellness

Good health is paramount to good living. Good health is something many people tend to appreciate only when it is deteriorating or gone. You can have millions of dollars in the bank, a beautiful house and a nice car, and it will mean nothing if you are sick. I never smoked, used drugs, or drank alcohol. Early in my adult life I had poor eating habits and did not exercise consistently. About the same time my kids were pre-teens, I started to make healthier choices in my life, including diet and exercise. My kids benefitted from this modeling. Today they are grown and for the most part, they read labels and are aware of the amount of sugar, carbohydrates and fiber in their diets and they are modeling healthy behavior and food choices with their children.

Legacy

How do I want to be remembered? In order of importance I rank myself as a "Father, Husband and Friend." Parenting is a serious job that requires unending sacrifice, patience and commitment. Fathers have a special role. I know that many children are being raised by hardworking single mothers. Many of these mothers are doing a great job and they need to be saluted. Despite their heroic efforts, there is no substitute for a father in a child's life, especially the bonds that are created between a father and his daughter.

My sons are fathers with daughters. I am so proud of them. They are kind and caring men who are highly active with their children, and that makes me enormously proud and happy. They are evolving from being fathers to being active dads.

Write down how you would like to be remembered after you leave this earth. Do not limit yourself while making your list.

_____

_____

_____

_____

_____

_____

_____

_____

_____

_____

_____

_____

_____

Final Thoughts

This chapter is your personal call to action! You are not reading this book by accident or chance. If you think you can improve as a father, it is never too late to be better.

My main reason for wanting to contribute to this project is to share the principles that have served me so well. Fatherhood is full of high and low moments.

As I write this chapter, the world is battling the COVID-19 pandemic. We are grappling with "new normals" and social distancing. The Shelter-In-Place and Centers for Disease Control Guidelines are creating stressors in our lives and communities. As bad as things are, this pandemic is also an **opportunity** for fathers to "step up" and be dads who spend more time with their children and families.

My dining room has become a makeshift classroom for my four-year-old granddaughter. Dads are having to be creative with games, online activities, indoor exercises and conversations with their children. Again, look at this crisis for what it is, but also look for the opportunities to spend time with your children.

When things get tough, you can rely on the principles and advice in this book to improve your life and the lives of your children. You are NOT alone. If you want to achieve success as a dad, you must be consistent and have faith.

Faith is the greatest power at your disposal. The only time you can fail is when you give up on faith, so incorporate faith as part of your success formula for being a great father.

I wake up each day with a sense of purpose. I know I can do great things for myself and my children.

Reflection Worksheets (If it's important, you will write it down).

1. Assess where you are as a father or dad today:

_____

_____

_____

_____

_____

2. After reading this portion of the book, I have learned, or was reminded:

_____

_____

_____

_____

_____

_____

3. I can use what I've learned in the following way(s):

_____

_____

_____

_____

_____

4. What is the personal and emotional cost of being away from my children?

_____

_____

_____

_____

_____

If you use the advice in this book, you will be a better father. I guarantee it. The principles are here. So what are you waiting for? If you are fortunate to have access to your children, don't take that situation for granted. Every moment that you do not spend time with your children is time that you cannot get back.

··

"My father didn't tell me how to live. He lived and let me watch him do it."

Clarence Budington Kelland

··

About the Visionary Author

Kimmoly K. LaBoo is a Published Author, International Speaker and Certified Master Life Coach. She is at the helm of LaBoo Publishing Enterprise, as CEO and founder. She is a highly respected change agent in her community and around the world.

Her award-winning company was created for the independent self-publisher. Kimmoly enjoys providing expert guidance and unlimited support to her clients, helping them recognize their brilliance, sharing their stories with the world, as writers.

She has dedicated her life to serving girls and women through mentoring, and coaching. Her compassionate coaching style, challenges clients to embrace change and show up confidently, using their unique gifts and talents to impact and serve others.

She was recently named among the Top 25 Women in Business by Courageous Woman magazine. She has appeared on Think Tech Hawaii, WPB Networks, Heaven 600 Radio, ABC2News, FOX5 News, and has graced many stages speaking and training to include, Department of Veterans Affairs, Blacks in Government National Training Conference, and Coppin State University.

Kimmoly is the mother of two amazing sons and currently resides in Baltimore, Maryland.

<u>**Contact Information**</u>:
www.laboopublishing.com
staff@laboopubishing.com